I0449274

The Natural World of Ivy Lane

The Natural World of Ivy Lane

Era S. VanDenburg

Copyright © 2010 by Era S. VanDenburg.

ISBN:	Hardcover	978-1-4535-3553-0
	Softcover	978-1-4535-3552-3

All rights reserved. No part of this book may be reproduced or transmitted in any form or by any means, electronic or mechanical, including photocopying, recording, or by any information storage and retrieval system, without permission in writing from the copyright owner.

This book was printed in the United States of America.

To order additional copies of this book, contact:
Xlibris Corporation
1-888-795-4274
www.Xlibris.com
Orders@Xlibris.com
66514

CONTENTS

BIRDS

MAMMALS

AND OTHER CREATURES

DEDICATION:

For "Van", scientist and gardener.
In memory of our son, Kurt.

THANKS TO:

Taniya Ann Fatticci for her computer, artistic and photographic skills; Julie A. DeLong for her artistic skill and patience; Karen V. Letcher for her assistance and faith in me; Catharine Brown, Mickey Cox, Paul Early, Dottie Promiscuo, Mary Putschi, and Valerie Schutsky for their criticism and friendship through the years; Scott Shalaway for his newspaper nature articles and his recommendation of good books to read.

To all those at Xlibris, for their understanding and patience, thank you.

Special thanks to illustrators:

Julie DeLong, cottontail rabbit
Taniya Fatticci, Carolina wren, cardinal, cedar waxwing, gray squirrel, red fox, raccoon, and American toad
Grant Lashbrook, house wren, ruby-throated hummingbird, yellow-breasted sapsucker, great horned owl, screech owl, broad-winged hawk migration, and Christmas count
Dale "Van" VanDenburg, striped skunk, whitetail deer, and monarch butterfly

Special thanks to photographers who provided the cover art:

Taniya Fatticci for the author photograph
John McNamara for the cover photograph of the red fox
Dale "Van" VanDenburg for the cover photos of the butterfly and sharp-shinned hawk

INTRODUCTION:

Perhaps more than anything else, my childhood on a farm is responsible for my interest in nature. Whether making mud pies or tagging along with an older brother to his catch-alive traps, I was a part of that fascinating outdoor world.

"There's an egret in the meadow," Mother would call. Or, "Look in the oak by the front porch, Era. The orioles are building their nest."

She showed me the scarlet tanager, foxfire in burning fireplace wood, and the most dazzling display of the northern lights I have ever seen. She and I sat on the steps at sunset, watching cloud formations of ships, palaces, or elephants, whatever suited my childish mind at the time.

Awareness of a much larger world developed when I began school, and yet it was still the natural one that held me spellbound. My jaunts through fields and woods continued until World War II interrupted, and I gave up that part of my life. That lasted only until I married an outdoorsman, and with my forest entomologist husband we've travelled many trails. They have led us to Ivy Lane, and within the pages of this book you will read about the wildlife that makes this place so special to us.

Some birds of Ivy Lane are year-round residents while others arrive in spring and leave in fall after having brought off their young. As they depart, those that have nested further north arrive to spend the winter, and in the case of the white-throated sparrow, linger well into spring. Of course all the migrants that appear do not remain. Some stay for a day, or maybe two, to feed and rest before hurrying on. We may see a single bird of an uncommon species for a few minutes only.

The mammals are different. Early on, gray squirrels claimed a share of the birds' food, and rabbits made a playground of the yard. Then one morning after a night's rain, unfamiliar muddy footprints criss-crossed the wet driveway. So, rabbits and squirrels were not the only four-footed animals on Ivy Lane, and soon one of those night prowlers checked out our back porch.

My husband continues to collect insects and even finds a new one occasionally, while butterflies and bees still visit the gloriosas planted by the previous owners.

Though changes have occurred on our one acre, they have not lessened our pleasure of living with our backyard wildlife.

BIRDS

House Wrens

Bugs in our garden in summer are in danger, for that is the season when "Jenny" and "Johnny" Wren are parents. All day long they carry creepy, crawly things to eat to their young in the birdhouse my husband built for them.

When I got up one morning at six o'clock, they were hard at work. While one caught a spider lurking on the eave of the garage, the other snatched a caterpillar from a petunia to take back to their hungry babies. Then they were off again to look for bugs and beetles.

Early settlers to America called the female house wren "Jenny" because she reminded them of their only wren back in Britain, which legend says was once the "King of Birds".

According to an ancient fable, all the birds in the world had gathered to choose as a ruler the one that could fly the highest. The mighty eagle soared into the air, far, far above the other birds. Certainly, he had won. But then a perky winter wren flew from its hiding place among the eagle's feathers. Singing loudly, it flew high above the tired eagle and earned for itself the title of King.

In our country, Cherokee Indians believed that wrens announced the birth of babies in the tribe. If the baby were a boy, the wrens were sad, for he would grow up to hunt them. If the baby were a girl, the wrens were happy, for little girls wouldn't harm them.

Of the ten species of wren found in the United States, the house wren is the most widespread, nesting all across this country and Canada. But when fall arrives, they leave their summer homes to spend winter with sun lovers farther south.

Wrens belong to the family Troglodytae, a word meaning "cave dwellers". While it is true that some nest in rock crevices, the marsh wren

---

prefers to build a nest of grass, leaves, and fine plant fibers attached to several reed stems. The rock wren places its nest on small flat stones in an animal's abandoned burrow, or a crevice in a cliff. A pathway of stones usually leads to the nest, and the bird may even pile tiny pebbles at the entrance. Other species nest in anything from a paper bag, to an old hat, to the clothespin bag hanging on the clothesline.

The house wren is in this latter group, using whatever is available including old woodpecker holes, abandoned hornet nests, rural mail boxes, or anything else people leave around. A small box, a basket, or a tin can will do. They are at home in urban settings as well as rural and suburban areas, adapting to conditions that might destroy another species.

The story of our house wrens began our first spring on Ivy Lane when our neighbor asked, "You don't have any wrens in your yard?"

House wrens nested in their birdhouses every year, often bringing off two broods, they told us. They loved the birds' bubbling song, which earned for the tiny songsters the Chippewa Indian name, O-du-na-mis-sug-ud-da-we'-shi, meaning "a big noise for its size".

That winter my husband built two wren birdhouses from scraps of lumber. The floor was 4x4 inches and the sides were 4x6 inches. The depth of the house from roof peak to floor was eight inches. He cut a one-inch diameter hole in the front about six inches above the floor. A larger entrance would permit house sparrows to use the box, and this we didn't want. We have since learned that an entrance about two inches long and one inch wide will permit wrens to enter more easily with nest building material.

The following spring, my husband placed one box about ten feet from the ground on a maple tree. He hung the other about six feet above the ground in a birch tree. It faced northeast while the first faced south.

Johnny stopped by in early May and inspected the second house inside and out, but he flew on over to our neighbor's where he had probably nested the year before. Sadly for us, our wren houses remained vacant.

Then about six weeks later, the same Johnny, or perhaps another, appeared. He sang his loud, boisterous song from the mimosa tree and the pussy willow. Between choruses, he pushed beaks full of tiny twigs into the wren house on the maple tree.

Suddenly, Jenny fluttered down to sit beside Johnny, but only for a second. With sweet whisperings, she entered the box. She popped back out, flew straight to the mimosa where Johnny waited and told him a thing or two, namely, I suppose, that he had provided poor nesting material and she would finish it herself.

Jenny chose her material with great care. Only feathers and the finest grass roots would do, but I have read that a wren nest once found was constructed of 188 nails, 4 tacks, 13 staples, 10 pins, 11 safety pins, 6 paper clips, 2 hooks, 3 garter fasteners, and a buckle.

When Jenny started brooding her seven eggs and was no longer free to flirt with Johnny, or follow him to the far end of the yard, he moved over to the other birdhouse.

"What's he doing?" I asked my husband, who was spying on Johnny with binoculars. He grinned and handed the glasses to me.

"Why, he's building another nest! That tongue-lashing Jenny gave him a few days ago didn't help a bit," I said.

"He's looking for Jenny number two," my husband said. "Or maybe it's three."

In fact, the male house wren may claim several nest sites in his territory by first removing any nesting material from the previous year. Then he proceeds to stuff twigs about four inches long into the box or cavity. When a female shows interest, he will escort her to his sites, and if she chooses one, she may remove the twigs he has so patiently placed in the nest.

Johnny, it turns out, is a philanderer, moving freely from one mate to another, but our Johnny was forced to remain faithful. All the female house wrens in our neighborhood were busy brooding eggs or tending babies, so Johnny sang away the 13 days until Jenny's eggs hatched. Then he began to help her feed their family.

As I watched the two tiny brown birds hurrying in and out of the box, I wondered how many insects the family would eat in our yard and garden before leaving in October. One male is known to have made 1,217 trips in a single day to feed his family.

Besides ridding our yard of a host of insects, the jaunty little birds have given us great pleasure. They have permitted us to peek into their private lives and have offered day-long symphonies, which would have pleased even Mozart.

CAROLINA WRENS

The house wren is not the only wren at Ivy Lane in the nesting season. The Carolina, the state bird of my native state, South Carolina, is a permanent resident, and his song can be heard even in winter.

We see the Carolina peering around the garage roof where he must find lots of insects, but in winter, he's a common diner at the suet log. Perhaps the suet enabled him to survive a severe winter recently. When snow is deep, the vivacious little bird that spends most of his time feeding near, or on, the ground, must find food elsewhere or starve. At such times in their northern-most territories, their numbers are almost decimated.

One fall we were surprised to find a Carolina sleeping on a corner brace under a metal window awning. I knew that place would be too cold in winter, and he would need to find a warmer one. A Carolina, at my sister's home in South Carolina, solved the question of his winter sleeping quarters in a simple way. He slept in a sock she had left hanging on a line on her porch. With the first real cold night, our wren deserted the awning for a warmer niche, I hoped.

According to Forbush and May in *A Natural History of American Birds of Eastern and Central North America*, the bird was once known as the "Great Carolina Wren", with emphasis on the Great. But Great was dropped from the name when larger wrens were discovered in the West. The Carolina remains the largest of the wrens in the eastern United States. At 5 ½ inches, it is 1½ inches longer than the smallest, the winter wren, which occasionally visits our yard in fall and winter.

Carolina wrens mate for life, and together they build a nest. They have nested in our upside down canoe, but they especially like the corner of our yard where the screened porch joins the dining room. They have nested beneath the window air conditioner, but one year we had not installed the conditioner as early as we usually did. In mid-June, Van called me. "Come and watch," he said. As I stepped to his side, a Carolina flew to the adjoining window with a fine dead grass stem in her beak. She added it to a nest on the windowsill where a storm window had been raised, but a screen had not been pulled down. We did not see a male that afternoon, and the nest was never completed.

Van and I are often amused at the antics of our wild family members, but I was more puzzled than amused when I walked up on our back porch, after an hour or so away, to find clothes pins strewn all over the floor. I picked them up and put them back in the open cloth bag, while I wondered aloud if a red squirrel was "getting back" at me for not filling his favorite feeder before I left.

"Could be," Van teased. Then he began to find clothes pins on the floor. Sometimes two or three, or even as many as seven, would be scattered clear across the porch, as if something had started to carry them away but changed its mind.

If we watched the porch, there was no activity, but if we took a rest after lunch, we were sure to see the culprit's activities had resumed. When a day passed and no pins littered the floor, we began to hope, and when two days passed and we didn't have to pick up pins, we decided that the red squirrel had forgiven us, but we were mistaken. I opened the door to find more pins almost lined up across the floor, and sticking out of the bag were sticks, pine needles, and bits of dry grass. I quickly closed the door, and as I did, a Carolina wren brought more nest material to add to that in the bag. This time, we never saw a female, and the nest was soon abandoned.

Another year, and both Carolina and house wrens were vying with each other for nest space on the back porch. The house wrens settled in a Christmas gift birdhouse, which had been covered with seeds when we received it. The Carolinas built their nest in the porch attic, after they found the air vent, and for days we were scolded by wrens if we opened the back door. So we waited, hoping to see the fledglings on their first flights. We did not. The Carolinas were earlier risers than we, and they didn't stay around to wait for our best wishes. The parents had hurried the young off to the shrubby tangle to learn the ways of the avian world.

Now, there was only one nest to watch, but already I was bothered by the actions of the male house wren. He would come to the lilac bush nearby, but he had no food in his beak. After sitting there for seconds, he would fly to the box, but I could not see the entrance from the kitchen door, so I never knew if he entered. Finally, he quit coming. In a few days, Van opened the box to find a nest with four tiny light brown eggs. Then we knew. Something had happened to "Mama", and as I held the beautiful little eggs in my hand there was a fleeting moment of sadness.

JUNCOS AND SPARROWS

It is late September, and Van and I keep watch of the backyard feeder area. We know it is time, or almost time, for the juncos and white-throated sparrows to arrive. They have nested north of us, and now we anxiously await their return.

Whether any of the first juncos to arrive will stay with us all winter, we do not know. How far have they traveled, and is this a rest stop only? It is possible that some, or even all, may continue their journey after resting and feeding. In other words, our yard may be a way station only for the early arrivals, while those appearing later may remain. However, from the first fall sightings, most often in October, as many as 25 of these well-known "snowbirds" are daily diners on our cracked corn and millet until they leave in April.

The juncos in our yard are fond of nijer seed also. We were expecting only goldfinches to be attracted to the small plastic seed holder with the tiny holes, but dropped seeds soon caught the eyes of other birds, especially juncos. They found that they could sit on the rods and eat directly from the feeder, and some winter days they outnumbered the finches.

A thud at the window alerted me late one cold afternoon. Bird Hit! I opened the door to see a male junco sitting on the patio, his head drooping. I scooped him up quickly with my hands and hurried back inside. Grabbing a shoebox, I put the little bird inside and placed the top on the box. With a knife, I slit some holes in the top, lifted it, and added a small jar lid of water to the box and a few grains of fine cracked corn. That was all I could do. I went to bed with little hope for the junco.

Next morning, I decided to peek in the box before removing the top. Surprise! Two bright eyes stared at me. Quickly closing the box, I hurried to the patio, removed the lid, and my stunned junco of the night before flew free into the winter world.

While the slate-colored, dark-eyed form is our common junco, two pink-sided Oregons, at one time considered a species, appeared in our yard one winter. With pink sides and back, they quickly caught our attention and were unusual western visitors for several days.

Juncos depart our yard for their nesting area in April, but one spring we noticed one had remained. When he was still here after a week, we began wondering why. He flew. He ate. He did not act sick. Then one day while feeding, he stood with his head directly toward us, and we realized why he was still here. His left wing drooped. He stayed until I began to believe that he might be going to remain, but on May 28th, we saw him for the last time.

Staying with us even later than the juncos is the white-throated sparrow, our longest staying winter resident. Arriving in October, while we are enjoying Indian summer, male white-throats are already in their winter "dress". The white head stripes are dull, but by the time they leave us in May, they are snowy white, and the stripe just above the eye has a bright yellow spot near the beak. We are sure to hear their song of, "Sow wheat, Peaverly, Peaverly," and we regret their going, but we also know that in five months they will be back. It's nature's way.

Once, in our yard, the appearance of a white-throat surprised us. An immature fed at the ash tree feeding area on June 10th, 31 days after the over-wintering flock had left. The bird did not seem to be in any stress as it ate that day, nor on the day following, but we did not see it on the 12th. We hoped that it had continued on, and that it would have a safe journey.

On a walk our first autumn here, a sparrow I did not recognize flew up into a sassafras bush a few feet in front of me. Upon checking our field guides, I knew without a doubt that it was an immature white-crowned sparrow. He, or one of his kind, soon found our back feeding area, and to our delight, he remained all winter. As spring advanced, his light tan head bands whitened, and by the time he left for his northern journey, he was a beautiful male in full mating plumage.

We look forward to the white-crowns' visits and also those of the species that follow. Sometimes arriving as early as October, *iliac*, the form of the fox sparrow in our area, is a rich brown. At seven inches, they and the white-crowns are the largest eastern sparrows. Some years they do not show up until mid-December. After staying a few days, they seek denser shelter or continue their movement farther south. Returning in March, we welcome them as one of our early northward bound migrants and listen for their beautiful song.

These are not all the sparrow species we have seen in our yard. Tree and field sparrows were common in earlier years, and a single swamp sparrow stopped in on April 28th, 1975, and the next day two Savannahs showed up. A pair of song sparrows lives on our acre, and it isn't too unusual to find a flock of chipping sparrows feeding on gum tree seeds in fall.

All add to our pleasure, and we welcome them.

Ruby-throated Hummingbird

July and August are the months when the ruby-throated hummingbird usually appears in our yard. With wings beating as many as 50 times a second, and a tiny heart pounding 1200 times a minute, the bird hovers at the pink phlox to snatch an insect or sip nectar with its long tongue. With speeds up to 30 miles per hour, the hummer flies away, leaving the phlox to check out our neighbor's red salvia.

Early European settlers in America were much taken with the "humbug", as some called the tiny bird, because his fast beating wings sounded like those of a "humble-bee".

Constant and frenzied activity requires the small bird, weighing about the same as a penny, to eat every few minutes. Though 60% of its food may be insects, it may consume half its body weight in sugar every day. A 170 pound man would burn up 155,000 calories a day were he to live a life equivalent to that of a hummingbird.

The ruby-throated, the only hummingbird found in the eastern United States, except for an occasional western vagrant, is the smallest bird found in our area, but he is quite able to take care of himself when danger threatens. With his swift flight he can easily outdistance his enemies, though he doesn't hesitate to tackle those such as a hawk or even an eagle if need be. His long, sharp bill is a formidable weapon, and Forbush called him a "mighty warrior". He is a mere 3¾ inches long, including the beak, yet three hummers in the western United States are even smaller. The Lucifer and Costa's are 3½ inches while the calliope is 3¼ inches. The bee, of Cuba, is only 2¼ inches long, the smallest bird known.

Male hummers are some of the most beautiful avian species on our continent. In poor light, the throat of the male ruby-throat appears black, but the slightest movement of the head can turn the throat into a flaming gorget, while the back shimmers with metallic green. The female is less colorful. Her throat is whitish, with none of the breath-taking flame of the males'.

While the female may appear in our yard earlier, it is most often August when the male ruby-throat arrives. He visits the feeder often, and I suspect that he is preparing for migration, which may take him to Central America. Males migrate earlier than females and young, and all may travel as much as 2000 miles, including a non-stop 500-mile flight across the Gulf of Mexico. To accomplish such a feat, the bird may gain half again its normal weight. After wintering in the tropics, where insects abound and a profusion of flowers bloom, offering plenty of nectar, they must make the return journey, arriving in Pennsylvania in April and May.

Males arrive back in the U.S. before females and claim territories. According to Charles Fergus in *Wildlife of Pennsylvania*, when a female approaches a male, he will perform "U" loops, believed to be defensive displays. Should she sit, he changes to "side-to-side" arcs, which may be his way of luring her with his red throat.

Not until 1937 was the speed of the ruby-throat known. John Bichard May, a photographer, had learned about a powerful new camera used in the Massachusetts Institute of Technology laboratory. He told his neighbors, Mr. and Mrs. Laurence J. Webster, about the camera. At their invitation, two professors from the Institute arrived with the camera. Their photographs showed that at 550 exposures per second, with the estimated duration of each exposure 1/100,000 part of a second, a hummingbird's wings beat 50-55 times per second when the bird is hovering and feeding.

The female alone builds the tiny nest, which may not be on the male's territory, but nearby. Weaving shredded bark and bits of plant fiber together, she attaches it to a tree limb with spider web. With lichens, she covers the entire nest, into which she lays two white pea-sized eggs. The eggs hatch in 14-16 days, and so tiny are the newly hatched nestlings that four can sit in a teaspoon.

The female is the sole defender of and provider for her young. She feeds them by thrusting her long beak down their throats and regurgitating semi-digested food. One female ruby-throat in Michigan was observed feeding one young in a nest and brooding two eggs in another nest about four feet away. One report stated that both nests were on the same limb.

—

Warblers

The first autumn we were on Ivy Lane, we found a small nest about two feet off the ground, tucked in a blackberry tangle in the brush field next to our back yard. Van thought the nest was that of the common yellow-throat, a small yellow warbler with the male sporting a black mask. I was delighted to think that warblers nested so close to our yard.

Though the warblers had already gone south for the winter, I began to study in our bird books the species found locally, in preparation for their return in the spring. Were any found in Pennsylvania that I had never seen? Might I see a cerulean?

"Oh, I hope so," I told Van. "There's even a record of a West Chester Bird Club member seeing, in the southern part of the county, the rarest warbler found in the United States."

Getting no response, I continued, "It's named for the man who discovered it at Cleveland, Ohio, your old haunts, in 1851."

"Kirtland's," he said. "Nests in Michigan and winters in the Bahamas," and then, "Really? Seen here? You aren't hoping to see that bird here, are you?"

"No. We'll go to Michigan to see Kirtland's," I said.

Many enthusiasts enjoy warblers more than any other group of birds. With such names as bay-breasted, black-throated blue, and golden-cheeked, one can understand why birders search streamsides and treetops, brushy tangles and weedy fields for the elusive, colorful birds. And, while several have the surname of their discoverers, three western species have the given names of women; Lucy's, Virginia's, and Grace's have that distinction. Also, two warblers share the names of American cities, that of Cape May, in New Jersey and Nashville, in Tennessee, while four are the same as that of states.

Three are Tennessee, Kentucky, and Louisiana, while the fourth was a life bird for me in our yard.

On an October day in 1984, a small bird moved cautiously through the asters beside the garage. I caught glimpses of pale yellow under parts and a dark back before he flew to the raspberry bed where he alighted on the ground and began walking. I gasped. The only small bird, with which I was familiar, that walked was the horned lark, and *That* bird, in the berry patch, was not a lark. Slowly and carefully, I eased closer and closer, all the time hoping he would not fly away. At last he turned his side to me, and I saw a grayish throat and a white circle around the eye. I knew at once that he was one of two warbler species I had never seen. I raced inside, when he disappeared into the berry vines, and grabbed my favorite bird guide, The National Geographic's *Field Guide to the Birds of North America*. There I found that the Connecticut warbler walks. The similar mourning and MacGillivray's do not. Those words assured me that I had seen a new bird to add to not only our yard list, but to my life list as well.

My lifer is more apt to be seen in Pennsylvania in autumn than in spring, but even then it is uncommon. It is a skulker, feeding on the ground and seeking out brushy tangles on its migrations. From its breeding ground in Canada and the upper region of the Mississippi Valley, the bird starts moving eastward in late summer, and alone travels southward, leaving the United States via Florida for South America. On its return the next spring, it migrates up the Mississippi Valley, seldom appearing in the Atlantic coastal states.

Of the 37 species of warblers reported in the annotated List of Chester County Birds, compiled by the West Chester Bird Club, we have seen 28 in our yard. Six of those have appeared only once to our knowledge. Others appeared often in spring and fall migrations, especially from 1972-1991, but not one showed up every year. The black-and-white was the most frequent, stopping by in all but five of those years.

The warblers returning in fall bear little resemblance, in some species, to those moving northward in spring. The male bay-breasted is a striking, small warbler sporting a chestnut cap, throat, and sides when he passes through our area in mid to late May. When one stopped in our ash tree on a September day, there was little of the rich chestnut on his sides and it was missing entirely from his head and throat.

Confusing as the adults are, the immature warblers of fall are even more so. There's not a cheep, chirp, tweet, or twirp to help me name that dull little gray-backed, twitching bird in the maple tree. Is he the same species as the one in the birch? Better look at his tail again. Is it longer? Does he have a white eye circle?

Yes, some continue southward unidentified.

Warblers

Of the 144 avian species seen in or over our yard, 28 are warblers.

1. blue-winged
2. golden-winged
3. Tennessee
4. Nashville
5. parula
6. yellow
7. chestnut-sided
8. Magnolia
9. Cape May
10. black-throated blue
11. yellow-rumped
12. black-throated green
13. blackburnian
14. pine
15. prairie
16. palm
17. bay-breasted
18. blackpoll
19. black and white
20. American redstart
21. ovenbird
22. Louisiana waterthrush
23. Kentucky
24. Connecticut
25. common yellow-throated
26. Wilson's
27. Canada
28. yellow-breasted chat

(Still to be seen: orange-crowned, yellow-throated, Kirtland's, cerulean, prothonotary, worm-eating, northern waterthrush, mourning, and hooded.)

CARDINALS

The stranger arrived at the back feeding area on September 22nd, 2006, and for the first seconds I saw the bird, I thought it was an exotic escaped from a zoo. Then it was gone, and Van was trying to tell me that I had seen only an immature bird.

"No. No," I was yelling. "It wasn't!" And then, "It's back. Look. It's by the weigela bush." Now, there was no more guessing. The stranger was a cardinal, but like no other we had ever seen. Why, the head was white, and so was the crest, but it had a red tip. And, oh my, there was a splotch of coral feathers on each light brown wing, and the breast was the normal color, too. At least the beak was orange like a normal cardinal's, and she gave food to a juvenile male cardinal. A female, we decided, but strangely albinistic.

A short while before, I had read about the strange coloration in some birds, and I knew that our visitor fitted that description, but I had forgotten the term. Within days, Dr. Scott Shalaway spoke to the West Chester Bird Club, and he kindly informed me of the correct term. The cardinal was leucistic. Once I would have called her a partial albino, but there are differences, better explained by a geneticist, I think, or an ornithologist.

We decided to call our newcomer Leu. Only once before had we named an animal in our yard, but Leu seemed a bit more sensible than calling her "that strange bird" every time we spoke of her.

Though we never saw the other cardinals attack her, Leu's visits were always short, and she came most often in the afternoons. As Van and I often watched for her, we talked about the avian possibilities for another year. Would a male accept her as his mate? Would there be offspring? What would they look like?

Gradually, her visits lengthened, and she sometimes fed on the ground with other birds. She began to appear more often, and once she dashed at another female cardinal in what looked like a half-hearted attempt to drive her away.

Autumn passed, and winter was almost over when a family illness called us away. After putting out extra food, we left, expecting to return in days, but days grew into weeks, and not until almost three weeks passed could we return. We hurried to fill feeders and spread cracked corn on the ground, but few birds returned to our yard. Eventually, the more common ones showed up, but only once did we see Leu after our return in late March of 2007.

The cardinal is the state bird of at least seven states: Illinois, Indiana, Kentucky, North Carolina, Ohio, Virginia, and West Virginia. Found in more than half the contiguous 48 states, it was once rare in Pennsylvania, but is now found north into Canada. It is one of our yard's resident species, with numbers fluctuating some years up to the twenties in winter. Though not a migratory bird, the cardinal may move from one area to another in search of food, which most likely accounts for the increased numbers in our yard some winters. Feeding well into dusk, they are known as the latest feeders of the day.

As early nesters, their first brood is often lost when spring storms batter the northern range of the species. A nest of young in our yard succumbed to a bitterly cold rain one spring.

April and May arrived, and the juncos and white-throated sparrows departed for more northern nesting areas. Replacing them were catbirds and house wrens arriving from the south. The first claimed the berry patch, while the wrens settled down to raise a family in Van's birdhouse near the garden. One pair of cardinals claimed the immediate yard area, and there were no spring storms to destroy their exposed, naked babies.

Summer came. August, with its heat and flying insects, made us look forward to cooler days in September. And then, Van called to me on September 13th that a cardinal, very much like Leu, was at the back feeder, but he had not seen the bird well enough to be sure. For several days, the identification remained a question, but finally a sighting in perfect light confirmed our hopes. It was Leu.

Then, just as she did the year before, she began coming more often to the back feeder. Her behavior was that of her earliest visits, cautious, or so it seemed to us, of the other birds. She did not eat in the feeder with other species, not even a chickadee. If she was in the feeder and another bird came, even a female cardinal, Leu flew away.

How old is Leu, and what is the average age for female cardinals? The fact that she fed a juvenile in the fall of 2006, supposing that it was her offspring, eliminates that year as her natal year, I believe. If that is true, she is at least two years old or more, having out-maneuvered the sharp-shinned hawk and other predators common in our area.

Will Leu remain with us for the summer of 2008; we began wondering as winter slowly crept toward spring. No. She did not. We saw her last on April 21st. But again, as in the previous two years, she appeared in September, 2008 on the 24th.

And now? From my journal: February 5th, 2009

"We have not seen Leu since January 2nd, when a severe ice storm occurred. She had never adjusted to the other feeding birds, though I never saw one bother her. It's possible she was not getting enough to eat to sustain her through such weather."

I remain watchful. Hoping.

Again, from my journal: October 17, 2009

"Leu did not return in Sept."

ROBINS

When we moved to Ivy Lane, the previous owners had left a birdbath, but to our amazement, birds did not use it. We watched, and though there were birds in the yard, only an occasional house sparrow visited the water. The visitors that did use it were the gray squirrels, and it wasn't long until the top lay in pieces, broken by the antics of the bushytails. We purchased another birdbath just like the old one, but the birds ignored it also.

Then one morning, "Look! Look!" I yelled to my husband as I stared out the kitchen window.

I had taken out compost material in an old, dark pan the previous evening, and on my return, I set it down in front of the garage door while I went to the mailbox. Important mail claimed my attention, and I forgot about the pan. During the night rain filled it, and now a song sparrow and a male cardinal splashed, while a catbird tried to snatch quick drinks.

My husband and I wondered why the birds were attracted to the water in the old pan but not the regular birdbath. Could it have been because the pan was on the ground? After all, that's where birds most often find water. Anyway, we have continued to use dark pans, and we continue to be as amused as we were the day we looked out to see our neighbor's mallard ducks trying to swim in our too-little pan. Our most astonishing experience, however, occurred on one late December afternoon.

Beginning at 3:12, and for an hour and 22 minutes, robins swarmed around the water. A half dozen, eight, ten, at the same time, drank not two or three sips, but for minutes each drank and drank. Occasionally, there was a minor squabble as one tried to push in before his turn, but for the most part, it was a well-behaved gathering. As one left, another took his place from those standing by, waiting a half-dozen deep.

While the robins drank, small birds did not come near the water, but a red-bellied woodpecker braved the throng to get a drink, the only time I've ever seen that species at the water. Several starlings, birds we had not seen in the yard for weeks, tried to "shoulder in", but robins kept arriving, seeming to drop from the ash tree by the dozen.

These birds were not bathing, splashing out the water, but drinking only, and when I caught a glimpse of the container, I was startled to see that it was almost empty. I hurried to take out a gallon of fresh water, the same amount I had put out in the morning. The robins merely flew into the trees and waited. By the time I returned to my place at the kitchen window, the birds were back, drinking.

Where had these thirsty birds come from, and why did they choose such a small water "hole" when we have so many streams and lakes in our area? We could only wonder.

For several days, robins continued to come for water, but not in the hundreds. Most often, four or five would arrive together. Their droppings, from the bittersweet berries they were consuming nearby, yellowed our driveway. When the food supply was exhausted, they moved on.

Two years later on another December day, robins descended on our yard after a four-inch snowfall. This time, instead of water, our holly tree claimed their attention, and in less time than it took the earlier flock to drink, these, though fewer, stripped the tree of almost every berry and left.

In early spring, or sometimes before the calendar date proclaims it, I will hear someone say, "I heard my first robin today." I too, listen for the robin's song, as have American's since early settlers saw and named the bird that reminded them of their English robin. A long-ago gentleman wrote that the robin's song expressed "love, contentment, anxiety, exultation, rage, and herein the robin seems more nearly human than any of its kind".

In June we are sure to hear the robins in our yard sing what must be that song of exultation, said to be that of the male when his mate's eggs have hatched, or are about to hatch. When I was a child, we said he was singing for rain.

Before March 4th, 1913, robins were considered game birds in some states, but on that date, the Federal Migratory Bird Law made the robin, along with other songbirds, a protected species.

Cedar Waxwings

". . . good natured, happy, tender-hearted, affectionate, and blessed with a good disposition." If you are wondering what person of the previous century, or any time for that matter, was thus described, you are off track. The perfect gentleman wasn't a person at all. It was a bird, the cedar waxwing, which ornithologist Edward H. Forbush was describing in an educational leaflet for the National Association of Audubon Societies. He also noted that the waxwings' "graceful form" gave it "an appearance of elegance . . . peculiarly its own," according to the book *Birds of America*, edited by T. Gilbert Pearson, another well-known ornithologist of the early 1900's.

Waxwings appear in our yard almost any season of the year, but most commonly in the winter and spring when they feed on holly berries, if the robins haven't eaten all of them. Their visits are never long, remaining a few hours or a day at the most. They are great roamers, always hurrying on.

One spring, much to our surprise, a pair remained when the flock moved on and soon began building a nest in a Japanese maple tree in our yard. This would be a chance to observe the nesting behavior of an uncommon area species, so we thought, but such was not to be. They deserted the nest, whether because of lawn mowing under the tree or the activities of such predators as crows, blue jays, and squirrels, we do not know. We also thought our yard a very unusual place in which to nest, as waxwings nest in loose colonies, often near streams.

Waxwings use various materials to build their nests. Animal wool, string, narrow strips of cloth, and an assorted variety of natural woodland fibers serve to safely hold the three to five eggs, which hatch in 12-13 days. Though hatching coincides with fruit ripening, the young are fed insects at first. The adults are adept at catching insects, reminding watchers of the true flycatchers. Later, the young are fed fruits. It is believed that sweet fruit serves as 80% of the food consumed by waxwings in the Northeast.

Waxwings are not aggressive toward each other as are some birds when feeding. They have been seen passing fruit, or even a caterpillar, back and forth. Acts of pair bonding are even more interesting. Two may be sitting near each other when one decides to hop even closer to the other, but he doesn't remain there. He takes a hop back, only to hop next to the other again, and hop back. Almost as if it is a game, the hopping back and forth may continue for some time. Mated waxwings are known to pass flower petals back and forth.

WOODPECKERS

Of the 175 woodpecker species found worldwide, 22 breed in the USA and Canada, and six of those, including the smallest, visit our yard. The downy is a mere mite in size when compared to the other five we see, but he is more tolerant of our presence. If he is on the suet log when we drive into the yard, he moves only to the back side of the log to continue feeding.

This woodpecker is 6¾ inches long from the tip of his beak to the tip of his tail, while at the other end of the scale the pileated is 16½ inches. We have never seen him in our yard, but once, as we sat on our patio enjoying a beautiful day and the singing birds, a pileated flew over.

During pioneer days, these magnificent birds were offered as food in markets, but Audubon, the bird artist, reported them to be "extremely unpalatable". They declined rapidly as early settlers cleared mature forests, but they were able to adjust to second growth forests, and, as a result, are fairly common today and sometimes visit suburban feeders.

Woodpeckers have a unique way of getting together. They drum, and many would-be late sleepers, and some not so late, have been roused out of bed by a drumming bird. The bird drums by striking its beak against a dead limb or tree. That is, unless it has found a more resonant sounding board as had a male yellow-shafted flicker at our neighbor's house. He used their drainpipe.

Drumming brings together the male and female for their courtship rituals. The rapidity and strength with which they hammer their beaks against a tree is truly amazing, and we wonder why their brains aren't addled. According to *Song and Garden Birds of North America*, by the National Geographic Society, thick skull bones and a specialized tongue structure prevent injury.

After much to-do, chasing each other through the trees and bobbing and swaying to each other, the couple settle down to nest building. If a previously used nest hole isn't available, the pair excavates a new one. Now, drumming serves to warn other woodpeckers that the territory is occupied.

The pileated may use the same drumming limb for years, but nesting is another matter. Usually, the bird chooses a dead snag high in the forest's leafy canopy well away from human areas. Chips as big as a man's hand fall to the ground as the birds chop out a nesting cavity with their chisel-like beaks, earning them the title of "Master Woodchopper". The same tree may be used for several years, but a new home is excavated each time. More than a bushel of chips littered the ground beneath one tree in Wisconsin, so I have read.

Woodpeckers eat a variety of foods, both insect and plant. With their extremely hard beaks, they chisel into trees and with very long tongues extract grubs and beetles. It has been estimated that ¾ of the animal food of downies and hairies consists of injurious tree insects, certainly a reason to encourage the birds to visit our yards.

An exception to the meat-eaters is the yellow-bellied sapsuckers with about half of their food vegetable matter. For years, they visited our yard in spring and fall. They secured sap by drilling ¼ inch holes in the trunk of a crabapple tree, the only tree in our yard they ever used, but according to Dr. Scott Shalaway, nature columnist, they are known to use 275 species of trees. They also eat poison ivy berries and, through the process of elimination, spread the obnoxious weed.

Though he is most often a suet feeder when we see him, the red-bellied woodpecker shares the sapsucker's love of plant matter, eating fruits, cultivated and wild, including oranges on the tree. One can imagine the frustration of orchardists upon finding their fruit destroyed by woodpeckers.

The yellow-shafted flicker is another woodpecker that visits our yard. The species has been called wood pigeon, high hole, and the name by which I as a child knew him, yellowhammer. It is the state bird of Alabama, and it is said that Civil War soldiers in the state marched off to war with a yellowhammer feather in their hats. We enjoy watching the flicker sunbathe in a dust pile in our yard, and we are glad he feasts on ants, though he, too, may be bringing the poison ivy seeds into our yard.

The adult redheaded woodpecker is a lovely bird, but we have seen only one in our yard, an immature. He tried vainly to cling to a metal clothesline pole on an autumn day. We wished him luck as he flew away. Just how far had he come and how much farther would he go, we wondered?

—

One day as I watched a downy at the suet log, I was surprised to see him fly away in a direction I had never seen one fly before. In minutes, a downy, I believed to be the same one, returned from that direction, grabbed a bit of suet, and flew back. Curious about his behavior, I called my husband, and we watched as the bird returned, grabbed more suet, and flew back. We were curious as to where he was going, so while Van watched the suet, I ran to the west end of our yard just in time to see the downy returning.

"He's back on the suet," Van called seconds later, and then, "He's gone.

There flew the downy across the west end of our yard, on over the highway, across one corner of a housing development, over a street, and on toward a woodlot. There was no doubt in our minds now. He had a family to feed, and he had found a generous food supply.

Downy babies are brooded for the first two weeks of life. The parents share in the task as they do during incubation, with the male brooding the nestlings at night.

The white and black markings of downies vary considerably, as I learned when a female appeared in the fall of 2003. She was very much like downies of the Rocky Mountains, which have more black than our eastern race. She visited the suet often that winter but disappeared in early March. We often wondered about her. Had she survived? If so, did she find a mate? Then to our surprise, in autumn, she (we like to think it was the same one) returned, and with her came a black male. As of this writing, April 2005, they are visiting the suet log daily.

WATER BIRDS: WOOD DUCKS
AND GREEN HERONS

It isn't unusual for us to see ducks and other water birds flying over as they move from one pond or lake to another. What really catches our attention is seeing them in our yard.

"There's a duck in the yard near the highway," Van called to me one morning. "Maybe a female. A wood duck," he called as I hurried out the front door.

It was a wood duck, but she wasn't alone. Fluffy little greenish ducklings scrambled through the grass, trying to keep up with her. Just how many she had, we were never sure, as she moved back and forth in a screen of hedges, but wood ducks may lay as many as 15 eggs.

Wood ducks nest in tree cavities as high as 60 feet above the ground. As we humans often settle down near the area of our birth, the female "summer duck" seeks a site to build her nest near where she was hatched, though "build" is hardly the correct word. She carries no material into the cavity but lays her eggs on rotted wood chips on which she has placed down from her breast. When the eggs hatch, she broods the young overnight, but the next day the ducklings, one by one, climb to the rim of the nest and bail out. Amazingly, few are injured as they hit the ground. As the nest may be some distance from a pond, lake, or stream, (this nest was at least a quarter mile) it is imperative that the mother start leading her brood immediately toward water, and that is what we were seeing. She had nested in a hole in a tree in a friend's yard two blocks away.

She alone had chosen the tree cavity, though she and her mate had become a pair while on migration. Perhaps they had wintered along a stream

—

in South Carolina or marshes of the Georgia coast, but when warmer winds arrived, she led him, thought to be the most beautiful duck, to the area most familiar to her. He protected her from the advances of other males well into the incubation period, but he deserted her before the eggs hatched, to join other drakes for his yearly molt. She alone would protect their ducklings, and the following year, if she survived, she would lead another male to the same nesting area, maybe even choosing the very same cavity.

Even stranger to me than seeing wood ducks in our yard was the visit of another bird associated with water. A harsh croak caused me to look up, and there in the top of a sycamore tree sat a green heron. In seconds he flew away over the trees, negating the name he is sometimes called, Fly-up-the-Creek.

Smallest of the herons, the green usually nests near water but may nest in dry woodlands, also. Unlike many of its relatives that nest in colonies, the green often nests alone, laying three to six eggs.

Perhaps no other bird has amazed humans with its fishing ability as has the green heron. Whether standing on a board or a limb extending over water, or lying flat on a log, as has been reported, the bird is adept at catching a meal of fish.

Of course I had hoped our visitor would return with a mate, if not to our yard, then to the finger of woods adjoining our yard, and find a suitable nesting site, but we never saw the heron again.

Great Horned Owls

Through my kitchen window I watched the crows diving toward the upper limbs of a spruce tree. Their raucous calls and actions clearly implied "predator".

"Must be the red-tailed hawk," I said to my husband, Van. We had seen the hawk in our East Goshen yard only a few days before, and we knew that the crows would not permit him to hang around. They would harass him until he left their area. Their squawks continued, so whatever they were tormenting, now, seemed determined to stay.

I slipped my binoculars around my neck, opened the door quietly, and walked slowly toward the noisemakers. The crows saw me at once and speeded up their attacks. They became more frenzied and bolder, striking closer at a thick clump of branches.

About 50 feet from the trees, I stopped, and as I raised my glasses, a great horned owl flew from the spruce. Never had I been so close to a great horned in flight. As the crows escorted the predator away, I realized why "great" is the first part of the species' name.

The wingspan of the great horned can reach five feet, and it can stand two feet tall. Yet, it drifts through the air as silently as a snowflake. It is this area's largest resident owl and is found all across the United States.

When we moved here 25 years ago, we heard screech and great horned owls often, sometimes in our yard, sometimes in nearby large wooded areas. One night, three of the latter carried on a lengthy hooting "conversation", perhaps to determine which one of the two males would win the female. Though the woods are now a residential development, the owls hold on; a species able to cope, to some extent, with the changing environment.

How far the crows chased the owl, I don't know, but we continued to get glimpses of one through the trees all spring as he tried to elude the crows. By then, we assumed that it was the male of a pair that had nested in a nearby township park the previous year. We heard him hoot often, and we hoped he had a mate.

Great horned owls are early nesters. The female may be found sitting on eggs, usually two, as early as late January. Often they use the old nests of red-tailed hawks, or even those of crows or squirrels. The eggs hatch in 28 days, but since they are not laid on consecutive days, one fuzzy white nestling is larger than the other. In six to seven weeks, the young leave the nest to sit on nearby branches, but the adults must continue to feed them. At 10-12 weeks of age, they are flying and must learn to fend for themselves.

Great horns often nest in an area for two or three years, occasionally four, provided prey is abundant. Early ornithologists had little good to say about the owl, remarking, "He feeds while others starve," and calling him an "executioner" and a "stealthy murderer". Charles Bendire, of the old school, reported a nest containing "a mouse, a young muskrat, two eels, four bullheads, a woodcock, four ruffed grouse, one rabbit, and eleven rats". While it is known that when food is plentiful, the owl may eat only the brains of its victims, the great horned is a protected species today, accepted as a devourer of great numbers of rodents and vermin.

Mice, voles, and rats make up a large share of the owl's prey, but rabbits playing in the moonlight may not escape. Snakes and great horns have been found in battle, and even the smelly skunk is not safe. In fact, it may be a favorite food of the "flying tiger". Some specimens in museums have continued to smell skunky for long periods of time.

One July evening of the year following the crow-owl episode, a neighbor hurried over to tell us that an owl was on the ground in our yard. "I think he's injured," the man said. "It looked as if he fell through the trees."

My husband hurried out to find a young great horned, head still fuzzy, standing goggle-eyed under our maple tree. He watched us as we watched him, and stayed long enough for me to call a friend two blocks away who came with his camera. Our grandson and his girlfriend arrived by car, and it was only then that the owl waddled and flopped to the garden, hopped over the fence, and made his way into the woods. By that time, we knew that Bubo and his mate had chosen our yard and the finger of woods behind us in which to bring up their family that year.

We went to bed, happy and content, with our thoughts of the owl family. What could top having a young great horned in our yard? We found out early the next day, for as Van made his morning tour of the yard, he heard a soft "cu, cu, cu", a sound he describes as much like the coo of a mourning dove or the "kuk" of the yellow-billed cuckoo, in the brushy tangle at the edge of the yard. He had found not one, but three young owls, or two young and an adult, as we could not see one well enough to be sure which it was.

By the time I joined my husband, the owlets were making short flights from trees to tangles, so we soon left them to learn their lesson, without which life for them would be impossible. They must have learned it well for we never saw them again, but two adults, the same pair, we assumed, were back early the next year. The male's high-pitched hoots and the female's lower hoots, at dusk from the northeast corner of the yard, let us know they were present. One, the male, I believe, often moved from a hidden day roost in a fir tree into the warm bright sun of late February afternoons. Our movements in the yard seemed to be of no concern to him.

We had hoped the owls would use an old crow nest in a pine tree nearer to our back door, but they chose another site farther away and we never saw the young.

SMALL OWLS

"I think we have an owl in your flicker box," I told Van one early November morning.

I had looked out our kitchen window just in time to see all the little birds take off from the feeders and a larger brown bird streak across the yard straight to the box on a maple tree. Wings fluttered at the entrance, and then the bird disappeared into the box. It did not come out.

That was strange. The only bird I had ever seen enter the box was a starling, and it flew out immediately. Van had erected the box two years earlier, with hopes that woodpeckers, especially flickers, would nest in it. They never accepted it. Only squirrels showed any real interest, and they merely enlarged the hole.

After breakfast, Van placed a stepladder against the tree so he could climb up and look into the box. All he saw were two small tufts of reddish feathers, but that was enough. A red phase screech owl was sleeping the day away in his box.

Exactly when the little owl moved in we didn't know, but it may have been the summer before, for Van had hurried in one August evening to say that one was calling nearby. That was good news as we had not heard one for a year or more, and here in our yard and garden "Screech" could dine on tiny four-legged creatures every night with little effort. We wouldn't care if he ate a house finch. Or two. Or three. In fact, we wished that we could show the owl their roost. Those pesky little birds can, and do, change their diet from insects and seeds to green vegetation, and our broccoli must rate a 10 with those nesting near us. They eat every head that isn't netted.

Eastern screech owls are red or gray, but ornithologists aren't sure why. Two reds, or a red and a gray, may produce offspring of both colors, or all of either color, but when two grays mate, all the owlets are gray. To further intrigue owl students, this dichromatic trait does not appear in the western screech found along the northwest coast, which is all gray or slightly brown.

The species often mates for life, and may nest in a sleeping cavity or box. The usual number of eggs is four to five, and males have been found sleeping with females during incubation, which lasts about 26 days. According to Brent's *Life Histories of North American Birds of Prey*, the newly-hatched young shiver, which may account for the name "shivering owl", once used commonly in the South. Just as strange is its present-day name, since few people claim to have heard a sound resembling a screech from the bird. The call usually heard can best be described as tremulous, and was often in the past considered an ill omen.

Even today, so some say, Cajuns along Louisiana's Bayou LaFourche get out of bed to turn their left shoe upside down when they hear a screech owl, supposedly a sure sign of death, or at least a misfortune. This, so they hope, stops the owl's wailing and cancels the omen.

Such beliefs are widespread. In Guatemala, a guide quickly informed our group after we had spotted an owl, "When you see an owl, that is good luck, but if you hear one, that is bad."

Sometimes at dusk, "our" little owl sat in his doorway watching for an unwary mouse or vole, we suspected, but we never heard him call. In early spring he deserted the box, perhaps to sleep near his incubating mate. Now, when screech owl trills send us hurrying outside in evening to listen, we like to think that it is one of his offspring.

Though the screech owl is small, seven to ten inches, it is not the smallest owl in the eastern United States. That honor belongs to the shy saw-whet owl, rarely seen except by those who search for it, or are lucky.

As the coffee perked one frosty December morning, I looked out my kitchen window just as a small dark bird, chased by a blue jay, alighted on the ground near the ash tree. Immediately, the jay attacked the sitting bird, which took wing, and with the jay chasing, the two flew to a hemlock tree in our neighbor's yard. In seconds I followed, for already I suspected that I had added a new bird to our yard list. As I approached the tree where the birds had alighted, the jay left, squawking his way back to our yard. I stared up into the tree, and looking down at me from a limb about eight feet above the ground was a tiny owl, only a smidgen bigger than a bluebird. I could hardly believe that I was seeing a saw-whet owl. And, he had been in our yard.

I checked on the owl several times during the day. Sometimes he slept, but often his eyes were open.

Ornithological literature is full of stories of people picking up the little owls, those sleeping or nesting. When early-day egg collectors raided a nest, often the female had to be removed by hand from the woodpecker hole serving as a nest chamber. If she did fly, she flew only to a nearby branch where she sat and stared at the human intruders.

The saw-whet lays four to six eggs. The female broods the owlets for about three weeks, after which she may leave the care of the young to the male. Since eggs are laid at two-day intervals, and hatch accordingly, older chicks may help feed their younger siblings, says Scott Weidensaul, noted author and bird bander.

The saw-whet is found over much of the U.S. but is often overlooked, for it spends its days sleeping in evergreen thickets or tangles. However, when Weidensaul banded the birds with radio transmitters, he found them, at least in the fall, sleeping in the "high outer branches of large oaks and maples" in the Appalachian Mountains of Pennsylvania. He believes the owl to be far more common than once thought, as he and his helpers netted as many as 1,000 in less than two months during one fall.

When I checked the Ivy Lane owl at dusk, he was gone. The next day was the Christmas Bird Count, and I hoped that he would return after his night of hunting, but he did not.

I've never seen another saw-whet in our yard, but I keep looking, and I hope that someday I'll hear the call that gave the small owl its name, a rasping sound like that of a saw being sharpened.

Sharp-shinned Hawks

When my husband and I began feeding birds, we created, unwittingly, a banquet table for a sharp-shinned hawk, one of three accipiters adept at catching small birds. The sharpie, about the size of a mourning dove, was trouble we hadn't expected, for he used our yard as his hunting ground all winter.

My first inclination was to shoo the demon (yes, that's what I called him) away by banging on the kitchen window, or racing out the door yelling and clapping my hands. I did neither, for the sharpie was like a ghost. He appeared and disappeared in seconds . . . until one December morning.

As I watched from the window, feeding birds exploded into nearby shrubbery and the weedy field, then froze in position. Not a head turned. Not a wing fluttered.

The sharp-shinned had swooped in low between the house and garage and struck at the early morning feeders. He missed his prey, even though the buildings had shielded his approach, but he had another tactic to fall back on. Without stopping, he flew to the maple tree at the far end of the yard and alighted on a branch about 25 feet from the ground. His long, barred, slightly notched tail, and bluish-gray back blended beautifully with the bare winter branches.

Not a single movement betrayed his presence as I watched him with binoculars, yet I knew that his sharp eyes were continuously scanning the yard and field. Then, like a feathered thunderbolt, he sailed down toward a leafless forsythia bush. A junco, perhaps an immature, had made a mistake. It was a slight error, just a tiny flip of a wing, but the sharpie had seen.

In *Birds of Prey of the World*, Grossman and Hamlet state that Peruvian Indian tribes in South America pay homage to the sharp-shinned for his keen eyesight, and now that visual acuity seemed about to pay off. The sharpie threaded his way into the bush, an ability that makes him an excellent hunter, but one that now slowed down his pursuit. That split second enabled the junco to escape, and the hawk was left to try his luck elsewhere.

I didn't see the sharp-shinned for a few days, and I guessed he was hunting in another territory, or had cleared out of the country. I hoped so, for by now I had claimed the cardinals, blue jays, and white-throated sparrows feeding in my yard, and I wanted the sharpie to keep the heck out. I remembered that even ornithologists had spoken out against the villain in the past because he preyed on small harmless birds. He was shot as a matter of course, or in one instance, trapped when he visited a poultry yard.

My mother had lost a considerable number of spring chicks to a raiding sharpie. While she was outside one day, he struck a fryer and killed it, but Mama's yells frightened him away. She reasoned that he would return, so quickly she built a trap and baited it with the dead chicken. The "blue darter", as she called him, returned, entered the trap, and, "I killed the scoundrel and had the chicken for my supper," she told me.

Sharp-shins nest over much of North America. They build a rather flat platform of sticks close to the trunk in coniferous trees. The well-concealed nest is so large that even the tail of the incubating bird may not be seen from below.

The four or five colorful, multi-patterned eggs hatch in about 21 days, and the young sharpies leave the nest when three to four weeks old. But before they are ready to fly, one characteristic of all bird hawks is evident. Females are larger than males. Thus, an adult female sharp-shinned may be as large as a male Cooper's hawk. This overlap in size can cause confusion when trying to separate the two species in poor light.

Young sharp-shins migrate south in early September with parent birds following later. They take advantage of wind currents created by hollows and hillsides to speed them on their way past such famous watching points as Cape May, New Jersey, Hawk Mountain, Pennsylvania, and Hawk Ridge Nature Preserve at Duluth, Minnesota.

Though some sharpies remain in the northern United States and Canada all winter, I hoped the one that came to our house was merely a late straggler who now was well on his way to Panama. It was not to be.

A grackle's terrified squawks from the bittersweet, honeysuckle tangle, as I went for the mail, destroyed the tranquility of the autumn week. There was the sharp-shin in hot pursuit of the frightened blackbird.

For the next few days we watched the hunter employ a number of new hunting tricks. Besides using buildings to shield his approach and his "wait and watch" strategy, he flew low over the field, pouncing unexpectedly upon his prey. When he missed, he continued through the brush, flapping his wings and hopping about until the terrorized birds he was after froze or took to the air. He was a formidable threat to the wintering songsters, and yet we watched him strike and miss time after time. Slowly, I warmed to the little fellow's efforts, and I sometimes wondered if the dashing, pint-sized predator didn't end the day hungry more often than not.

Then, on January 23rd, snow began piling up at the rate of an inch an hour. I made numerous trips out to sweep off feeders and replenish the fast-disappearing supply of cracked corn and sunflower seed. At 4 PM, I made my last run for the day, and then watched from the window as the wee avian creatures stoked their tiny furnaces for the long, cold night ahead.

Suddenly, he was there. Where he came from, I never knew—only that one moment a beautiful male cardinal was alive—the next, he lay dying in the claws of the sharp-shinned.

I stared at the hawk. He looked around as if he expected danger. Maybe larger birds of prey had stolen his meals in the past. After assuring himself that all was well, he began to tear at the warm flesh with his powerful beak.

From somewhere deep inside my tensed body, an understanding surfaced. It wasn't "my cardinal" the sharpie was eating. The truth is, the red bird was more his than mine. He had killed to satisfy hunger, to prolong life. He had a place in the scheme of things, and his method of killing, though not pretty, was swift, efficient, and for a purpose.

I finally accepted what should have been clear all along—that there's a price to pay, emotionally, for feeding birds. I'll never interfere when a sharp-shinned comes to our yard. We feed the other birds. They feed the sharpie.

I turned from the window to begin my own supper.

RAPTOR MIGRATION

"Ninety-one, ninety-two, ninety-three," I counted.

That day, September 16th, 1984, began for my husband and me as most days did in mid-September. We had eaten breakfast, worked the puzzle in the paper, and then checked to see if deer had raided the garden the night before. The last gave us a chance to scan the autumn sky for migrating hawks, especially the broad-winged, smallest of the buteos. A few red-tails, perhaps recognized more easily than any other hawk in the United States, and kestrels, smallest of the falcons, hurried by singly, but not one broad-wing. The sky was devoid of the "show-stealers" as the broad-winged has been called.

We ate lunch outside that day, as usual, with binoculars by our sides. Noontime is a quiet time in our yard, and September 16th was no exception. By early afternoon we had almost given up. Not even a blue jay or cardinal visited the feeder. Still we watched, and in mid-afternoon we were rewarded with broad-wings forming kettles above our heads.

Van rushed to the east end of the yard and called back to me that as far as he could see, hawks were moving southward. As far as I could see to the west, hawks were on the move, also. Broad-wings were everywhere we looked. Before one kettle broke up above us, another was forming. Never had we seen so many hawks.

I continued counting. At 100 I held down my little finger, my ring finger at 200, the middle finger at 300. Realizing that I wasn't counting every hawk, that I could NOT count every hawk, I finally snatched off my binoculars and enjoyed the show.

How many broad-wings passed over our house that afternoon we do not know, but when the last one disappeared we had counted 1018, the most we ever counted on a single day. The next day, 584 moved through.

A few stragglers the next five days pushed the total count for September 16th through September 22nd to 1680. Once, in 1981, we had beaten that last number by three, but the high-count day was of only 852 broad-wings.

With the passing of the majority of the broad-wings, other migrants hurried along. Harriers, once known as marsh hawks, and even an occasional bald eagle, hurried southward. We saw an osprey carrying his fish in his talons. Those beautiful flyers, with kinks in their wings, have made a dramatic comeback in the past few years as has the bald eagle.

As October arrived, the number of sharp-shinned hawks increased. Unlike the broad-wings, this smallest of the three accipiters, or bird hawks, flies alone. Some spend the winter in this area and are terrorists at many feeders, including ours. One finds the ash tree feeder area an excellent hunting ground. He uses the garage to shield his approach to snatch an unsuspecting cardinal or mourning dove.

Another migrant, that is also a winter visitor to our yard, is the red-shouldered hawk, but instead of looking for small birds, he goes after small mammals. On a winter day, a male sat for 35 minutes on the bar from which hangs our nijer feeder. He continually peered at the ivy around the patio, and when he finally dropped down, I suspect that a mouse or vole served as a warm snack on the cold day.

During the ten years plus of watching raptors migrating over Ivy Lane, we saw 15 of the 16 species that are regularly seen at Hawk Mountain less than 100 miles north of us. Cold fronts to the north start these birds moving southward, and while every autumn day was not a "hawk" day for us, it was certainly worth the effort to spend time each day in mid-September and early October gazing up. With an unobstructed view to the north, we were rewarded often with the sight of raptor migrants winging their way to Mexico, Central America, and even farther.

In the early nineties, the number of hawks migrating over our yard declined. No more kettles of broad-wings formed. No more sharpies and ospreys hurried by. In 1995, we did not see a single bird of prey soaring southward. The autumn skies were clear, wiped clean, except for an occasional monarch butterfly, and so they have remained.

Today manned checkpoints across Pennsylvania and along the Atlantic coast report thousands of raptor migrants every fall. There was a time, however, when men gathered at checkpoints for another reason. Instead of binoculars, they carried guns. One such area was the Kittatinny Ridge near Kempton, Pennsylvania, where gunners gathered every fall to shoot any hawk flying past. Eagles, buteos, and falcons—all were shot and left to decay. But even then, there were men who knew the ecological and esthetic value of America's birds of prey.

———

Dr. Richard Pough, a Pennsylvania journalist and ornithologist who visited the mountain in the fall of 1932, was appalled at the destruction of these birds. He notified the Emergency Conservation Commission, headed by Mrs. Rosaline Edge. The determined woman set in motion plans to stop the wholesale slaughter of the birds, which led to the establishment of Hawk Mountain, the world's first raptor sanctuary.

Raptor Migration Data

Three Years When Number of Broad-wings
Counted Exceeded 1,000 Individuals

Year	1981	1984	1985
Total # Broad-wings Counted	1,683	1,681	1,480
High Count Date	9/10/81	9/16/84	9/12/85
High Count Date Broad-wing #	852	1,018	840

—

CHRISTMAS BIRD COUNT

"Stay out of cold wind," the doctor had ordered, but that would not be easy for me to do in December. The Christmas Bird Count season was only a few days in the future and I wanted to participate in at least two counts. Now, the doctor's orders threatened my desires. After much thought, I finally acknowledged that I would have to make changes and accept the fact that the 1988 count would be different for my husband and me.

For almost 20 years, I had jumped out of bed long before sun-up, made coffee, yelled at my husband to hurry, grabbed sandwiches made the night before, and raced to a territory to count birds on that special day. Now, the doctor's orders required that I stay inside, and I knew that I should accept his judgment.

Instead of participating in two counts, I decided we would participate in the West Chester, Pennsylvania Bird Club count only, counting birds coming to our feeders and those flying over our yard. We wouldn't have to get up as early as in previous years, I reminded Van, as we live in the count circle.

The West Chester Bird Club was formally organized in 1910, and thus, it is one of the oldest continually active bird clubs in the country. Its aim was to secure a vitally interested and congenial group.

The club was a serious study group, as evidenced by its activities. Life histories of species were written and reported on by members at meetings. Bird skins and eggs were often on display, and the club traveled by trolley, train, ferry, and whatever means was required to reach birding areas as far away as the New Jersey shore.

Soon after organizing, the club held its first Christmas Bird Count, a practice that continues, and on the designated December morning in 1988 I was ready with paper and pen. It wasn't surprising that the first bird to appear was a junco. The "snow bird" of my youth is a species that is with us from early autumn till mid spring. Next was a northern cardinal, a year-round resident who "cheer, cheer" cheers us up when we are tired of winter storms and spring is yet to come.

About that time Van joined me, and with his coffee, he settled down in the dining room to watch through the window the back feeder area and a portion of the bittersweet, wild rose tangle.

"I'll call out the names of the species as they come in," he said. "You eat breakfast and keep the list," and he began. "Tufted Titmouse," he called and quickly followed with Carolina chickadee, white-throated sparrow, another winter resident, and mourning dove.

The list continued to grow with crows, blue jays, and even a lone pheasant. Then a lull in the activity gave us time to get a second cup of coffee and speculate on just how many species we might get for the count in our yard.

"Do you think we'll get 20?" I asked Van, hopefully.

"Well maybe," he said. I knew he was doubtful. "Where are the house finches and woodpeckers?" he asked. "We haven't seen a goose yet. Nor a song sparrow. They're usually feeding by now."

Minutes later our count list number was creeping up and we became more hopeful, but as usual, mid-day brought another lull in the avian activity and made a good count more unlikely. We had 14 species on our list when we quit racing from window to door and back to window to eat lunch.

Though short of our goal of 20 species, when visibility failed in late afternoon we had counted 17 species in our yard. The next year we did better, seeing 21 species. While four we had seen the first year did not appear, we added eight new ones. The total number of species seen in the yard on Christmas Count days was 29. (See lists at end of chapter.)

As for the total number of birds seen, I have no idea, but I suppose the juncos and white-throated sparrows outnumber the others. Often we see a single bird of a species, and it's even possible that the ring-billed gull, seen in 1989, is the only one we have seen on our yard counts.

When we turned in our list to the area's lead counter, we realized how much we had enjoyed counting the birds in our yard and that we had remained warm, dry and out of the wind all day.

Tidbits

One winter day, I made red raspberry jelly instead of jam. Thinking that birds might like the seeds, I dumped them on a stump. It wasn't long until I looked out to see not cardinals and house finches enjoying my offering, but an accipiter, Cooper's hawk, sitting on the stump. Evidently, he had misidentified the red seed mass as gore and came in to prey on it. What a disappointment he must have experienced, for in minutes he left, even the yard, to do his hunting elsewhere.

For an hour and 50 minutes after we first saw him, the accipiter sat, hardly moving his head, even as the sun slipped westward and a tree shadow passed over him.

The sharp-shinned faced the sun from a dead limb three feet above the ground. Hardly a trace of his rusty breast feathers could be detected so fluffed were they against the bitter cold. Nearby on a patch of recently fallen snow lay a spot of red, unidentified even with binoculars.

Juncos and white-throats, somehow knowing that he was not hunting, returned to their feeding area 15 feet away. Watchful. Alert.

When at last the sharpie took wing, my husband hurried out to examine the remains of the victim. Tiny bones, picked clean as if scraped with a knife, lay on the snow. Not a feather identified the hawk's life-sustaining morsel.

As Van stood on the driveway one morning a sharp-shinned hawk struck at a female cardinal feeding on the ground about 15 feet away. The bird escaped by flying into a nearby barberry bush. The accipiter went after her, and for seconds Van thought she would escape, but whatever delayed her didn't deter the sharpie. He came out of the bush holding the cardinal, dropped to the ground, and immediately began to pluck the victim's feathers. About that time I joined Van, and so intent and immature was the predator that he continued to prepare his meal. Not until Van moved a step closer did the young sharpie fly away to finally consume what I imagine was his late morning breakfast.

One spring day after a night of showers, I was walking to the garden when I spied a chipping sparrow sitting just off the path. His eyes were closed and his head drooped as if he were expiring. I stopped and stooped down. The tiny bird barely opened an eye, disregarding my presence otherwise. Was he sick, hungry, or tired from a long flight, I wondered? I placed fine cracked corn in front of him. I didn't know what the outcome would be, but I had to leave him and continue my vegetable gathering. How long he had been there, of course I didn't know, but when I checked later, he was eating. Shortly afterwards, he recovered and flew away. I hoped his journey was almost over, though we would have welcomed him to our yard.

Only seeing the Connecticut warbler in our yard surprised me more than seeing a shrike and witnessing the savagery of the bird as he beat to death a tiny songster on our driveway.

At that time, what is now a bittersweet and rose tangle was an overgrown field of weeds and blackberries extending to a working farm with fields divided by hedgerows. Such open country is preferred by shrikes and is typical of that in which I had often seen the loggerhead in the Carolinas, but this was Pennsylvania, and it was January. So, was the one I saw a loggerhead or a northern? To be honest, I was not sure, though I have read that winter shrikes in this area are most apt to be northerns.

After seeing that morning performance, I understood the name by which the shrike was once commonly known, butcherbird. Perhaps he was really hungry because we found no larder tree in which he hangs excess food to be eaten later.

The 20-year Yard Christmas Bird Count

Total Species Seen in Count	Date Bird was Observed		
	12/19/1988	12/1989	12/20/2008
Dark-eyed Junco	✓	✓	✓
Northern Cardinal	✓	✓	✓
Tufted Titmouse	✓	✓	✓
Carolina Chickadee	✓	✓	✓
White-throated Sparrow	✓	✓	✓
Mourning Dove	✓	✓	✓
House Finch	✓	✓	✓
Red-breasted Nuthatch		✓	
American Crow	✓	✓	✓
Blue Jay	✓	✓	✓
American Goldfinch	✓	✓	✓
Downy Woodpecker	✓	✓	✓
Red-bellied Woodpecker		✓	✓
Canada Goose	✓	✓	
Northern Mockingbird	✓		
Ring-necked Pheasant	✓		
Song Sparrow	✓	✓	✓
Turkey Vulture			✓
American Robin	✓		
Red-tailed Hawk	✓		
Carolina Wren			✓
White-breasted Nuthatch			✓
Rufous-sided Towhee		✓	
European Starling		✓	
Sharp-shinned Hawk		✓	
Ring-billed Gull		✓	✓
Eastern Screech-owl		✓	
Northern Flicker		✓	
Fox Sparrow		✓	
House Sparrow		✓	
Hairy Woodpecker			✓
Total 31	17	23	15

MAMMALS

MY HUSBAND'S GARDEN

When my husband, Van, retired I wondered if he would start playing golf. "Isn't that what most retirees do?" I asked.

"I don't know," he said, "but I'm going to be a gardener," never realizing that his garden would produce far more than vegetables.

By the next spring, he had brought in a neighbor with a tractor to plow up the east end of our yard. Next, came trucks with mushroom soil, which was laboriously spread and spaded into the raw earth. Soon after, we planted various seeds, and when the carrots were four to five inches tall he informed me that we had to put up a fence. "Rabbits have found the carrots, and deer have clipped off the mountain laurel. They'll find the garden, too."

So, we fenced, planted, weeded, and harvested. "Twenty-six different vegetables," my sister said when she came to visit from South Carolina. "I counted them," she added.

We ate, canned, and froze peas and beans, cabbage and spinach, beets and peppers, turnips and eggplant, okra, cucumbers, and tomatoes. The list went on and on. And we shared with neighbors.

"People will start running the other way when they see you coming," Van said. "Everybody gets tired of zucchini."

"Don't plant so many," I said. "Just two hills next year," and I saw in my mind a smaller garden to weed. That was not the case, I soon learned.

"What's a garden without corn?" he asked. "We have to plant corn, but first I'll have to enlarge the space. Add another 10x20 feet, half again of what we already have. That will give us enough, and we can even plant winter squash."

So, he enlarged the garden, and we decorated the entire fence with strands of hair the barber saved for him. Hair is supposed to exude human

---

59

scent to repel deer, and we did get most of the corn, but the deer in our area are all too familiar with mankind odors. They got their share of corn, also, and through the years, so have raccoons and squirrels. One day, I found a woodchuck climbing the fence, and we've suspected skunks of sampling young sweet ears as well, but none found the garden so *Right* as did the rabbits.

Every day for more than two weeks one summer, we found a rabbit in the garden. Each day we chased Peter out, and when my husband found where he had slipped under the fence, he staked it down. But next day, Peter was back, so Van walked the entire fence, staking down and closing every little hole.

"Now, we'll see who wins this round," he said, as he grinned and brushed dirt from his hands.

Next morning, without a rabbit thought, we opened the gate, and so fast we hardly saw what happened, a rabbit jumped from the onion bed to the top of the fence. Holding on with his feet for a second or two, he teetered, and then sailed off the two feet high fence onto the grass, running.

"What the—," Van began, but he never finished. Huddled between two rows of onions, in the zoysia grass clippings he used for mulch, was a nest full of baby bunnies.

"That's not Peter, Mopsy, nor Flopsy," I said.

We quickly retreated to undo the stakes. Mother could go and come to the garden as she pleased. We would share our vegetables, and to our amazement, the damage was minimal; our pleasure, tremendous.

For three years, every summer, bunnies raced and played in the garden, sometimes exploding from under a cabbage we were about to cut or from the beans when I was picking them. But a year came when we saw no bunnies at all. More years followed, and there were no little brown puffs of fur to delight us. Still my husband saved the zoysia grass clippings. "Just for the onions," he said.

Then this past winter, a rabbit came every evening to eat grain we put out for the birds. In early spring, a second rabbit appeared. We watched in wonder as their courtship developed. The male would dash toward the doe that jumped straight up in the air while he ran underneath her. In his book *From Laurel Hill to Siler's Bog*, author John K. Terres tells of watching a pair of mating rabbits, and though he did not see it, he learned that the female sprays the male with urine when he passes underneath her. Mating, we knew, followed these energetic performances, but we never saw the final act. That it did occur, we have proof. One morning my husband came in, all smiles.

"We've baby bunnies in the onion patch," he said.

—

BUNNY

It's dusk, and the birds are feeding for the last time before the day ends. Three rabbits have joined them. They, too, eat the cracked corn and then go in search of "greens". Their salad, Van says. They seem to especially enjoy the wild aster leaves and those of the red raspberries, which are nearby.

The first rabbit to appear was smaller than the other two. Was he the young one Van evicted from the garden earlier this year? So well had the female concealed her nest, at the end of the onion row where dill had volunteered, that we had not known it was there until "Bunny" (we saw only one) began eating our fall broccoli plants. Van caught him, and while he squalled, put him outside in a flower bed. For days we saw him nibbling grass and clover as we walked to the garden, and then he disappeared. But not for long!

We began feeding the birds in August. The summer had been so dry, I was sure that wild plants had not produced enough seeds to support the residents, let alone the migrants. Within hours after filling the feeders, doves, cardinals, chickadees, and other birds were busily feeding on sunflower seeds and cracked corn. And there was Bunny.

The little cottontail rabbit often joined the avian flock, and for days he used the area as an exercise arena as well as a dining hall. Suddenly, for no reason that we could fathom, he would run across the back yard, circle, and return to his starting point. As days passed, he gradually lengthened his runs, sometimes veering into the tangle at the far end of the yard on his last race.

As Bunny ate one morning, an adult rabbit appeared, and I wondered as I watched just what would happen if they came face to face. I didn't have long to wait. Each fed toward the other, seemingly unconcerned. Occasionally, each lifted his head, but neither showed alarm. And then, when only inches apart, each raised his head, and they touched noses just for an instant. Then each hopped away to continue eating.

Was the adult Bunny's mother? Did he retain enough of his "baby" odor for her to recognize him? I don't know. Nor do I know whether the act of touching noses had any meaning at all to the animals, but to me, it was a moment I like to remember.

More About Rabbits

When we put mesh over the blueberries to keep out the birds, we decided to put the vinyl deer fence around the garden as well. We almost patted each other on the back as we finished the job. Why, we were even ahead of schedule. The corn was only knee-high. One year, deer had feasted on the juicy ears the night before we planned to pick them. Since then, we had put up the deer fence when the ears were forming. This year, there was another reason to put up the fence early. A woodchuck had found our peas and lettuce to his liking, so the deer fence would form a higher barrier and prevent the chuck's raids. It didn't, and we never did find his entrance.

But, there can be a price to pay for being so smart, and before many days that price was paid. Instead of dropping sacks of leaf mulch over the fence as we had done previously, each one had to be brought from the far end of the yard, past the garden to the gate, and back into the garden. My husband struggled, but as I spread the mulch, I kept one thing in mind. Zoysia grass clippings were for the onions, but mother rabbit would not be able to get in this year, as she had in the past to have her young. But surprises aren't unusual at Ivy Lane.

When we went to the garden to pick peas some days later, a young bunny nibbled grass in the pea row. We chased him out the open gate, wondering how he got in, but two days later, he was at the edge of the onions next to the peas. As I stood watching him, I heard Van say, "Well, how did you get in?" and he wasn't looking at the young rabbit.

I joined him to see what he was looking at, and there between the pea rows sat an adult rabbit. Van shook the peas. She, for I was sure in my mind that it was a female, did not move. Not until Van stepped toward her did she bound away across the onion bed and out through the fence.

—

"I'll see about that hole in the fence," Van said, turning off the tiller and tramping out of the garden.

"She may have babies in the onions," I said.

"We haven't seen her in here before, so I doubt it," Van said as he continued on his mission.

Outside the garden he found that she had chewed a hole in the vinyl deer fence where there was an old hole in the wire fence. He closed the deer fence hole and came back into the garden just in time to see a baby bunny scramble through another hole in the fence. Then, we saw not just THAT bunny, but a nest of bunnies in the onion bed.

Van picked up the tiller and we hurried out of the garden, but we couldn't just walk away.

"He's too tiny to be out of the nest," I said, "and he isn't weaned yet," I added as we walked around outside the garden looking for the little escapee. Van's sharp eyes spied him at once. About three feet from the fence, he was snuggled down in the grass, his little ears lying flat against his head. Slowly, Van crept forward, picked him up in his hands and took him back to his birthplace in the garden.

Next day, we did not see a bunny until Van went to the garden at dusk to read the rain gauge. There, to his surprise and pleasure, was Mama Cottontail with five bunnies.

"They were in a little ball, squirming and wiggling. Mama dashed off but only a few feet," he said.

When we got back to the garden, the mother was still there with the babies, only a couple of feet from where Van saw them earlier.

"She must have been nursing them when I first got here," he said. "I wish I had seen that."

I wish he had, too.

Bushytails, Flyers, and Fairy Diddles

There are those who believe that the riflemen of the Revolutionary War had perfected their skill earlier by hunting "bushytails", the eastern gray squirrel. That may not be as far-fetched as it first sounds.

Victor Cahalane, in *Mammals of North America*, likens the squirrels at that time to "swarms of grasshoppers", destroying the colonists' crops. Since pot-hunters alone could not control squirrel numbers, Pennsylvania put a bounty on the squirrels and in 1749 the state treasurer paid three pence each for 640,000.

There seemed no respite from the problems created by the small rodents, except when they, like Arctic lemmings, deserted an area. Since the travelers were always fat, naturalists believed that the migration treks had nothing to do with food but were the result of over population.

One cold, dreary day, I looked out to see the most bedraggled, thin squirrel I've ever seen eating sunflower seeds on one of our platform feeders. He remained the entire afternoon and left only when night arrived.

We thought it strange that no other squirrel tried to chase him away. They knew he was there. They simply ignored him.

Next morning, the little stranger arrived soon after I got up, and again, the resident bushytails overlooked him as he continued to stuff himself. That afternoon, he began to notice the other squirrels and his surroundings, sometimes sitting for short periods of time without eating. For several days, we watched the resident squirrels permit the little fellow to eat more than his share and gradually accept him as a yard mate. The starving, skinny creature that had appeared at our feeder grew fat and sassy with a clean coat and finally, a beautiful, bushy tail.

Some people go to great lengths to get rid of the pesky bushytail thieves. A friend spray-painted a squirrel's tail and hauled him to a park two miles away. Before the week was over, the squirrel had returned. Other friends had been live-trapping the little rodents at their feeder and releasing them in woods at the end of their street. They were beating her husband back home, the woman told me, so on a late fall morning she took one five miles away and dumped him.

"Now I feel terrible," she said when I met her later that day. "He may not find enough to eat this winter."

As our gray squirrel population increased steadily, my husband decided that it was time to bar the rodents from one feeder. I had suspected all along that sunflower seeds were disappearing from feeders at night. Then, on several nights, we found our outdoor light on and the suet log swinging wildly from the ash limb. I wondered what was going on out there. An opossum? Raccoon? No. Neither could escape so quickly. So, what was raiding the bird feeders after dark? I wondered.

One night my husband was late filling the suet log, and as he stood to hang the log back on its wire hook, a flying object sailed by his head, missing it by inches only. Startled almost to the point of falling off the ladder, he whirled around to see a flying squirrel clinging to the ash tree.

The night raider was another squirrel.

The flying squirrel is an expert glider, rather than a flyer, and may easily cover distances up to 100 feet. Folds of skin extend between his hind and front legs, which, when extended at right angles to his body, enable him to "fly".

These agile flyers are seen less often than are gray squirrels because they are nocturnal, but soft chirps in the darkness may alert one to their presence. Empty nut shells with tiny rough circular holes at the stem or blossom end is another sign of their presence.

Mother flying squirrels are devoted to their young, and when danger threatens, they go to almost any means to protect them. Cahalane reported that after a den tree was felled, one mother climbed up the clothing of the logger and rescued her babies one by one from his hands. Grasping each by the belly skin, she climbed a tree and then glided to another where she placed them in a new cavity.

We hoped that the flying squirrels would claim a flicker box Van had placed nearby, but our hopes were dashed when a family of mice took possession. However, we were not through with squirrels.

—

"We've a new visitor at the bird feeder," my husband said one November morning as he stood watching out the kitchen window. "A red squirrel just came in."

Eric the Red, as Van quickly dubbed him, stayed just long enough to stuff his tummy with sunflower seeds before swinging off through the trees. But the next day he was back. And the next, though he never stayed long.

Then one morning, the swaying of small maple branches caught my eye, and there was Eric. He had arrived much earlier than usual. One leap from the maple tree took him into the crabapple tree, and another jump landed him in the ash tree. Head-first, down the trunk he ran to the ground where he began eating, and Eric remained all day.

"Looks like our visitor has taken up residency," I said to Van a few days later.

"So I've noticed, and we may wish he hadn't," Van said.

I could hardly believe that. Why, Eric was special! He was so cute. I could laugh just looking at him, but as winter approached, Eric took on a decidedly different personality. Relentlessly, he chased away the gray squirrels. Morning, noon, and late afternoon, Eric was there, guarding the ash tree feeders.

Only once did we see a gray stand up to him. The gray came in, unseen by Eric while he was taking a nap. When he awoke and dashed down the tree to chase away the intruder, the gray faced him. Eric stopped short of physical contact, ran off a few feet, and tried again. The gray merely faced him again. Clearly, this was behavior Eric wasn't used to. He made two more half-hearted attempts to run the gray away, then gave up.

"Maybe he'll leave them alone now," Van said. "He's such a nuisance. I guess we'll have to get rid of him."

"No. You can't do that," I said, knowing full well that things would have to get far worse before Van carried out his threats. "One of these days he'll be sitting on top of the feeder and a hawk will grab him."

In the South, the red squirrel is a "boomer". Westerners call him a "chickaree," or pine squirrel, while some West Virginians call him a "fairy diddle".

Diddle, according to Webster, means colloquially, to "move jerkily up and down, or back and forth; to jiggle", and Eric seemed to do all those things at once. He would leap from tree to feeder and back to tree, race to the ground, and back up the tree as if conducting special morning exercises.

Not only were the gray squirrels chased from the feeding area, they were not even permitted in the east end of the yard. Even the birds were aware of Eric. He would race through a flock of juncos and cardinals for the sheer joy of putting them to flight, or so it seemed to us. As he sat on his favorite snag one day, Van saw him reach out and snatch a tail feather from a passing house finch.

Winter arrived, and Eric remained. January brought ice and snow, and Eric continued his watch, sitting hunched against the tree trunk; the chance of a hawk catching him was rather slim. The little rascal had adopted an ingenious escape plan, and it took only seconds to put it in action.

"Come here," Van called from the kitchen the day after a ten inch snow. He was looking out the window when I hurried in from the dining room.

"Watch Eric," he said.

The little squirrel was busy as usual in the area we had cleared of snow around the feeder. Then he was gone, though he had not run across the snow to a tree. He had suddenly disappeared.

"Now, watch the maple beyond the patio," Van said, and no sooner had he spoken than a red squirrel appeared at the base of the tree.

"Oh, no. There are two," I moaned for I did not want another Eric.

"No. It's Eric," Van said. "Keep watching."

I stood staring as the little escape artist ran up the tree trunk, along and over branches, and ran back down to the snow only to disappear again. In seconds, he popped out of the snow in the feeding area, scattering birds in all directions.

I could hardly believe what I had just seen, but after watching several repeat performances of what looked like pure play, I had to admit that Eric had bulldozed a snow tunnel 25 feet long.

In *Mammals of Pennsylvania*, by Doutt, Happenstall, and Guilday, I found that red squirrels do, indeed, burrow into the snow. Tunnels have been found more than 100 feet long, some with small rooms in which they store food.

So Eric was not an eccentric. He was just an ordinary red squirrel.

Later in the afternoon, Van and I investigated Eric's hide-away. The tunnel entrance at the feeder area was about three inches in diameter, straight for four or five inches, and then it veered to the left, which prevented us from seeing any further. It was about two inches off the ground, not on the ground as I had thought it would be. But one question remains. How did Eric keep on course underneath the snow to the maple tree?

They're an interesting and entertaining lot, these bushytails, flyers and fairy diddles. We don't begrudge them a few sunflower seeds any more. They offer us a close look at wild animals going about their daily lives while providing us with many hours of pleasure.

MICE

We have never kept birdfeed in our basement. Never. Never, ever. But we have found it there.

A spare rolled up rug lay across the arms of an old rocking chair, one end almost touching the floor. When we found a use for it and started to unroll it, a neat little pile of cracked corn lay inside the upper end.

"Mouse," my husband said.

"How?" I answered. "The corn is on the back porch."

"In his cheek pouches," my husband said.

"We don't have pocket mice," I reminded him. "They're in the West. Remember the one we found deceased in Texas?"

"Of course I do," my husband replied, "but our mice have pouches, too. Only thing different, they're inside the mouth, and they are not lined with fur."

"Well, wouldn't the corn have gotten wet and molded?" I asked.

"Apparently not," my husband of 58 years answered.

Still not convinced, I kept on talking. "But it's a long way from here to the back porch. How did he find the way?"

"Maybe the same way the snake did," Van said.

Enough said. I didn't want to remember that day.

There have been other mouse encounters, and all have not been in the basement.

One day Van told me that he had heard a strange noise the night before. "As if a marble was rolling across the floor," he said.

"Couldn't be," I said. "We don't have marbles." But a day or so later a pecan lay on our bedroom rug . . .

"Where did it come from?" I asked, bewildered, and wondering if we had been bewitched. My patient husband said, "Better check the bag of pecans."

A cousin in South Carolina had given us a generous supply of pecans the fall before, and we had placed the bag in a bedroom closet.

"The closet door is shut, so they can't be coming from there," I vouched. "And any way, what is moving them? Can't be a mouse."

I had a lot to learn.

There came a night when I too heard a strange noise, and slipping out of bed, quietly took a flashlight from my bedside table and made my way across the bedroom. Upon reaching the door, I turned on the flashlight, shining it on the bare hallway floor. Trembling and staring up at me sat the pecan thief, a wee house mouse with his treasure an inch or so in front of his nose.

Next morning, a pecan lay on the floor of the library, but a search of the room turned up no more. None, that is, until I noticed the cabinet door open. The floor of the wall cabinet was about four inches off the floor, and on it was a pecan.

"What . . ." I began, then hushed as I sat down on the floor, and reaching my hand to the back of the cabinet, I felt not one pecan but a pile of pecans.

Astonished, I sat there, and as I pulled out pecans, I tried to figure out how a mouse had moved those nuts up a four inch wide board to take them through the open cabinet door. I never did. I could only suppose that he held them in his mouth.

Years later, I had a reason to remove some books from the cabinet next to the one the mouse had used as a storage den. Can you imagine what I found? Yes, 29 pecans tucked neatly on and behind books.

House mice continue to invade our home every autumn. Most often they appear in the basement, but they never bother the bags of flour and sugar, cookies, or pasta. They're decent little visitors unless they find a way to the kitchen. That's off limits, forbidden territory, and they are not permitted to stay.

The white-footed mouse inhabits our area also and is often found in the garden, or nearby. One day as Van fertilized a blueberry bush, he uncovered a mother and her young. Quickly, he recovered them with the nest material and came to get me. By the time we arrived, Mom was already moving the babies, one by one, to an old rotting stump nearby. When she removed the last of her litter of five, she returned one more time to search well the nest area. Finding no more babies, she rushed back to the stump and disappeared. We left the area and hoped that she and her babies would adjust quickly, and well, to their new home.

RED FOX

Years ago a neighbor hurried in one afternoon to say, "Era, there's a fox in your yard. I've never seen one, but I know that's what it is."

It was. A red fox. He was nosing around a brush pile from which probably emanated rabbit odors.

When my brother visited sometime later, he and I went for a walk along the edge of the farmer's field at the end of Ivy Lane. As we neared a hedge row of sassafras, dogwood, and crabapple separating two fields, a red fox emerged from hiding and trotted away from us. A typical place to see the fox, we agreed, as Reynard prefers the more open spaces than does the gray fox, which likes more forested areas.

Time passed and Van informed me that foxes had a den on the church property adjoining ours. Red foxes are known to den in open fields, under old farm buildings, or they may choose to repair an old woodchuck burrow as did this pair. They mate in January and February, and the young, usually four or five, are born 51 days later. The male, or dog fox, provides for his mate, the vixen, while she tends the kits, by bringing her whatever he can catch or scrounge from garbage heaps and dumps. Later, both will hunt to feed the young, but by mid-June, the kits are weaned and following the parents on hunting trips. They may deprive the rabbit hunter of his quarry, but they serve the farmer well by consuming great numbers of mice, voles, and even insects. Snakes, turtles, frogs, fruits, and berries, foxes dine on all.

In July the young begin hunting on their own, and by autumn the males have deserted the territory of their parents, but the females may remain and even help care for their mother's young the next spring.

We kept our distance from the church property den area as we did not want to disturb the animals, and by late July our hopes of seeing the young hunters began to fade.

August arrived, summer moved toward fall, and not a single fox appeared. Then in late September, as Van and I sat on the back porch simply enjoying a quiet evening, a red fox trotted along the back edge of the yard. He was a large fox, beautifully furred. That was the first of many sightings, and soon we were seeing a red fox often in the yard, most times in the morning. Usually he came from toward our neighbor's yard across the street and trotted across the east end of our yard. Once he carried a small animal in his mouth.

Sightings increased, and we became concerned for their safety with so much daytime activity. We were almost sure that we were seeing two different foxes, but was it a mated pair or two young hanging around the old territory?

One morning as I watched from the kitchen window, a fox appeared in the east end of the yard, trotted by the ash tree, crossed the driveway, continued between the house and garage, and stopped to pee on my clothes line post. A male! No guess work this time. But was the other one a female?

Sightings continued. Christmas passed, and I had more interesting things to talk about than the weather, for on a sunny, cold morning, two red foxes trotted together eastward in our yard.

"They're mates," we almost shouted at each other, and we began guessing. Maybe they will use the old den, and we'll see the kits this year. Our hopes soared.

Then one morning, as I closed the refrigerator door, I looked out the back door just as the rear end and tail of a fox disappeared from my view, and he was running. I had never seen one run, so I knew something was amiss. I dashed to the window to see where he was going. He crossed our yard and Ivy Lane, still running, but stopped in the east end of our neighbor's yard and looked back our way. Then he continued on behind their house.

No doubt about it. The fox was afraid. As I hurried to tell my husband, I wondered what could have happened to frighten the animal, and at my husband's suggestion, I looked out the dining room window to check our back yard. No one was there. A short while later, a fox trotted, as one often did, from the east end of our yard, stopped on the driveway, and looked as if he were wondering which way to go—into the back yard from which a fox, most likely he, had run minutes before, or down the driveway. He chose the last and disappeared after crossing the west end of our neighbor's yard.

We had never seen a fox in the west end of the yards, so that seemed a bit strange, but an even stranger happening was to come.

—

As Van looked out the dining room window, a fox, limping and favoring the right rear leg, moved slowly through the tangle bordering our back yard and disappeared behind the garage.

Could the frightened fox be the one that had returned a few minutes before, and was he searching for the injured one? So many questions to which I have no answers, but I believe it was.

Months passed in which we did not see a fox, and I became fearful that they had left our area. Then when our daughter visited in July of the following year, she saw a fox near our compost pile. I was happy to know that at least one fox was in our area, but there were more fox surprises.

On a mid-August evening, two foxes, one smaller than the other, appeared in the ash tree feeder area where they nosed around. After some minutes, the smaller lay down, the two nuzzled each other, and the larger trotted across our driveway and out of my sight. Some minutes passed before he, or she, returned to the one waiting curled up as if about to take a nap. After the two greeted each other, the larger fox left again, trotting northeast through the yard and passing behind the garage.

By then, I had decided that this was a parent teaching a kit the ways of the wild, though I had read that the young are hunting alone by August. After some minutes, the kit arose and followed the parent.

Next evening, to my amazement, there was almost a repeat performance, but the following two days only the parent came. Maybe the kit had learned his lessons well and could finally catch his own prey.

Raccoon

"Yes, Sir. You'll catch him with this," the clerk assured Van, who was purchasing a catch-alive trap. "Just bait it with an apple and he'll go right in. Apple is a favorite of 'chucks," he ended.

Van came home, rummaged in the fridge until he found an apple, and set his trap right where he had seen the woodchuck that morning. Since they are day feeders, he checked the trap at dark, but it was just as he had left it. And so it was next morning.

"Maybe he was just passing through the yard," I said to my husband. "You'll probably never see him again."

"I doubt that," he said. "He'll be back, so I'm keeping the trap set," and he did.

Next morning I heard him calling me shortly after he stepped outside. "Come and see what we caught," he said, grinning, and there in the trap was an animal whose tracks we had seen in our yard.

"It appears that raccoons like apples, also," I said as I peered at the fidgeting animal. Van released him, and he left, hurriedly, for the nearest brushy cover.

The raccoon is a common mammal in Pennsylvania. Van caught a smaller one a few days later, and their muddy, little paws continue to leave tracks often on our driveway. They are travelers of darkness, and while supposedly preferring marshes and creek borders, they have adjusted well to our populated areas.

Procyon lotor contributed notably to the welfare of the pioneers as he had to Native Americans. He was hunted and trapped for his fur, and his meat was often served at the dinner table. The skins were sold, and the oil from fat was used as a lubricant for machinery and leather goods.

Raccoons are not true hibernators as are woodchucks, but when the temperature dips to 25 degrees or lower, they den up. They sleep soundly, sometimes for weeks, but their temperature and heart rate do not fall drastically.

There is no doubt that the raccoon's preference for wild, wet areas has to do with their choice of foods such as fish and frogs, but humans have contributed considerably to their diet. They are fond of our cultivated fruits and berries, as well as the wild ones, and many gardeners, including my husband, have awakened to find their ready to harvest sweet corn almost completely stripped of its shucks and half eaten.

Maybe someday biologists will agree on why raccoons "wash" their food. As for those that sometimes visit Ivy Lane, I don't think that it's a requirement. The only thing we have ever found in the water was a small bone, well cleaned of any meat.

Naturalists are changing their ideas also about the behavior of wild animals. They may not as yet term courtship "romantic" among the four-legged kind, but certainly February stirs wild blood much as Valentine's Day triggers human passion. Snow may cover the ground a foot deep, but ardor forces many woodland creatures out of their warm dens and hollows to go "a courtin'". On such nightly forays, the raccoon, with strange sounds, can surprise even an experienced woodman. Chirping, screeching, hissing, and growling, he is often able to protect himself.

The female is choosy about the mate she accepts. Just any old "coon" won't do, yet once they have mated, he goes his way in search of other females. The female is the sole provider and protector of her two to six youngsters that are born about two months later, wearing fuzzy coats and already sporting a mask.

By fall, the young are on their own, though they continue to sleep with their mother the first winter. Even pregnant daughters sleep with their mother.

And no, Van did not catch a woodchuck that year.

Opossum

A cold rain beat down steadily as I hurried from my car up the back steps of my home, to stop immediately as I stepped on my back porch. Was I seeing things? What was an opossum doing sitting on the bird food box?

"Oh, you poor thing," I said softly. "You've been forced from your bed by this awful rain. But don't get frightened and run away. I'll go to the other door," and I rushed back through the downpour and around the corner of the house to my front door.

I don't think the 'possum had any intentions of going back out into the rain. Perhaps he would have set perfectly still for me to walk by him, but I didn't know. I wanted him to stay where he was nice and dry. After all, he was the first opossum we had seen at our home, and I wanted him to remain until my husband came home from work. I was glad he would be in before dark, as opossums are more active at night because it is then they go foraging for food. And what an omnivore *Didelphis marsupialis* is!

This little short legged, pointed nose animal consumes everything he can get his little paws on. Dead animals found along roads are a special treat, and he devours large numbers of insects, toads, frogs, fruits, and vegetables. He is especially fond of young corn in the milk stage, and he may have shared our sweet corn during summer. The southern farm boy baited his catch-alive boxes with baked sweet potatoes when he trapped the small animals for their fur years ago. Enormous numbers were supposedly caught in the thirties, and they are noted furbearers, even today, for hunters and trappers in some states.

The species has changed little during its time on earth, which dates back to the Eocene period 58-36 million years ago. It is the only North American marsupial, an adult that carries its young in a pouch. At birth, the tiny embryo-like creatures, likened in size to a bumblebee, crawl into

---

76

the marsupium and fasten onto one of the 13 teats. If the number of babies exceeds the number of teats, the late comers are doomed. The lucky ones hang on for about two months and are on their own in about three. During the last days of their mother's protective care, they may ride piggy-back by holding onto her fur.

Because the gestation period is so short, only 12-13 days, opossums may have two or even three broods each year. Young have been found in a pouch in February.

Opossums use fallen trees with hollows, woodchuck burrows, or openings in rocky cliffs in which to build a cozy bed. They have an ingenious way of carrying leaves to the site, and they know how to do this at an early age. They gather the material one mouthful at the time, tuck it on their prehensile tail, which is held between their hind legs, coil the tail over the leaves, and proceed on their short legs to drag the entire load of several mouthfuls to the den.

When the weather is extremely cold and rough, Didelphis may relax at home for several days, but he is not a hibernator. He is soon out scrounging for anything edible, even though he runs the risk of getting frostbitten ears and tail, which are hairless.

Opossums have enemies on the ground and from the skies. All the larger predatory animals, including the red fox that visits our yard, and the great horned owls that have made Ivy Lane a major hunting ground, will attack an opossum. While their defense tactic, that of playing dead, may not save them from the hungry hunter, it is interesting to man. They fall on their sides, become limp, grin widely with tongue lolling out, and shut their eyes. This is believed to be a true state of shock, for the pulse and heartbeat of the frightened creatures are reduced, but as soon as the enemy leaves, 'Possum gets up and hurries away.

When my husband returned home from work at dusk, our visitor was still enjoying his dry abode, but a cardboard box filled with nice soft rags and a plate of food we put out for him were not appreciated. He scorned both and left under cover of darkness, to wander by night his own paths, I suppose, and by morning light, return to his own living quarters.

STRIPED SKUNK

"Something was in the corn last night, probably a raccoon," my husband said after returning from his usual morning stroll through the yard and garden. "I think I'll set the catch-alive trap tonight."

We had a small patch of corn, and when I went out to look I found several stalks had been pulled down, the young ears partially stripped of their shucks and the fresh kernels eaten. One or two more nights of such visits and we would never know if we liked Golden Bantam corn.

Van set his trap just outside the first row of corn, and I went to bed thinking that all the animals wandering Ivy Lane yards were much too smart to walk into a box. Wrong! Early next morning when I went outside to feed the birds, I noticed that the trap door had been tripped. I rushed over to take a look, but when I peered into the box, I retreated much faster than I had approached. Instead of a squirrel or raccoon as I expected, a skunk lay curled up, fast asleep.

"What an animal," I said to Van after I hurried inside to tell him. "He's in a trap, and he is so unconcerned about it that takes a nap."

I was the one concerned. "Watch what you're doing," I cautioned my husband as he went out the door. "Please, don't get sprayed."

After seeing how docile the animal appeared, Van poked him awake with a long pole and lifted the trap door. The skunk walked out and sauntered off into the scrub tangle without even a look at the juicy corn or Van. No doubt he soon found another bed, but I've often wondered if he might not have slept the day away in the box if Van had only opened the trap door without poking him awake.

Happily for us, there were no more raids on our corn, and it was delicious.

The striped skunk continues to visit our yard but always under the cover of darkness. We don't have to see him to know he has been about. We find his muddy, little tracks on our driveway after he has been digging for grubs in our lawn. He is not overly particular about his diet. He consumes large numbers of mice, and the eggs and young of ground-nesting birds are not safe from the hungry hunter. In summer he adds variety with wild berries, but the sluggish crickets and grasshoppers of fall supply him with the extra fat required for a long winter sleep.

Mephitis may sleep in an old woodchuck burrow, or he may dig one for himself. He may not be alone, either. As many as 15 have been found snoozing together. This is not true hibernation, but a torpid state in which the body temperature may fall as much as ten degrees, according to Charles Fergus in *Wildlife of Pennsylvania and the Northeast*. The skunk may wander about looking for food during mild weather, but in February his journeys are for a different reason. It's mating time, and it is most often at this time of year that our sense of smell alerts us to the fact that the wanderer is prowling our yard. When the skunk is threatened, he sprays, accurately up to 15 feet, his perceived enemy with a formidable musk, likened by Fergus to "skim milk with curds". Even the tiny naked babies are born with musk, and they know how to use it when eight days old.

The vile spray is a powerful means of protection for the small black and white animal, but some predators, such as bobcats and coyotes, are able to ignore it. Great horned owls are not deterred and may be the skunk's greatest enemy, even though they are rendered helpless at times.

J. Christopher Heil, a ranger and wildlife specialist with the Pennsylvania state park system, once told me of an owl-skunk encounter. A lady reported a "sick" or "injured" owl beside a park road. Heil went to the site and found a dead skunk and a great horned owl apparently suffering from the skunk's spray.

One night I awoke to our bedroom reeking of skunk. Something had upset our visitor close by. Very close by, and in minutes a great horned hooted in the gum tree just outside our window. Was he feasting on the skunk, or had his efforts been thwarted?

We'll never know, but skunks continue to visit our yard, and we welcome them. They destroy large numbers of insects and their larvae. We don't mind their malodorous spray when it is diluted by some distance, but when I have to close the doors and windows, I wish they would appreciate visiting rights to our yard.

WOODCHUCKS

There may be a few old-timers who believe still that if the woodchuck sees his shadow on February 2nd, we will have six more weeks of winter. It's best to forget that. The groundhog, woodchuck, or whistle pig, is not to be trusted as a weather prophet, and one can't even be sure he is sane if we judge all by an Indiana 'chuck. After a blizzard in 1978 when the temperature hovered around zero, that grizzled oldster decided that it was time to get up. On February 2nd or 3rd, he emerged from his burrow and left a mound of fresh earth on the snow.

Actually, the woodchuck's intentions are not to check on the weather, but to get the jump on other males, for as soon as they emerge from the burrow, males go in search of females. Fights break out when one wanders onto another's territory, and the result is chewed ears, shortened tails, and ripped hides.

When the male finds a female and mating is accomplished, he usually travels on, seeking other females, though one may stay with his first conquest for some time if she doesn't drive him away. Females have been known to move out and leave their consort.

Two to six young, tiny, blind, and naked, are born about a month later. By the time they are a month old, the young 'chucks are nibbling new grass at the entrance to the den. They are playful, but "childhood" for a woodchuck is of short duration. By mid-summer they are all on their own. They move into nearby shallow burrows in which to sleep at night and nap during the day, when not eating. They are most vulnerable to predators at this stage, both the wild kind and man.

Where food is plentiful, woodchucks remain near their burrows during the summer. Their territories may overlap, and they are seen often eating within a few feet of each other. There is no time now for the aggressive behavior exhibited during the mating season. Each 'chuck is too busy feasting on summer grasses, clover, dandelions, or the farmer's hay crop. They also eat fruit, sometimes climbing and damaging a tree to reach it, and they often get into trouble by raiding gardens.

When the woodchuck starts visiting our garden, my husband pulls out his catch-alive trap. How far a 'chuck will travel after being taken away and released, we don't know. Most we have seen in our yard looked to be youngsters of the year, but since we have never marked one, we have no way of knowing whether one ever returned.

Several years after moving here, I sat reading outside one day when movement at my right alerted me that something was near. To my surprise, it was a woodchuck, the first we had seen in the yard. When I got up to go inside, he didn't run away, though he was barely six feet from me. Nor did he run when my son went out and took photos. He remained unperturbed as he ate his way across a narrow stretch of grass, out of the yard, and disappeared into a wild tangle of vines.

For years we didn't see another woodchuck, but good things often come to an end too soon, and so it was with the 'chuck's absence. Almost as if he had surveyed the garden and knew exactly where his favorite vegetable had been planted, one entered, and in minutes devoured half a row of green beans.

"I refuse to let woodchucks eat my vegetables," Van said, and off he went with his trap. Had he not trapped the rodent, the 'chuck probably would have eaten more vegetables than we.

As days grow shorter and nights cooler, woodchucks grow sluggish, and about mid-October here in Pennsylvania, they are ready for a long sleep. Occasionally, a young one may wander around much later looking for the right site to dig its burrow. The winter burrow is an extensive maze of rooms and tunnels, in one of which the animal prepares its bed of dry grass. With its head between its back legs and its front paws around its shoulders, it sinks into a deep sleep. Its breath is shallow, pulse weak, and the body temperature may drop as low as 43 degrees.

In this inert condition, known as hibernation, the woodchuck spends the winter. That is, unless he is an early riser like the Indiana 'chuck.

—

Whitetail Deer

They saunter across the yard during the day. Sometimes one, sometimes two, or as many as seven may stroll across Ivy Lane from our yard to our neighbor's. They amble along the edge of the yard, snipping a twig here, a flower there, into another neighbor's yard adjoining ours. A doe and her fawn, or even two fawns, stroll by as we sit on the back porch at dusk. A spike buck appears from behind the garage, checks the daisies at the back door to see if any are to his liking. Van yells at him and he runs. Two deer, one with a six point rack, stare at us but show no concern before walking on. They are whitetail deer that have been pushed by development into our yards. Thousands are killed by hunters and motorists every year in Pennsylvania, yet the number in the state is believed to be in the millions.

To Native Americans and pioneers, wild venison was an important part of their food. It was sold in the early markets and so were the hides of deer. In 1721, Pennsylvania passed its first game law. This was supposed to protect deer for the first six months of the year, but few people paid any attention to the law. Nor did they obey a law passed in 1873 prohibiting the use of dogs for hunting deer. Not until the establishment of the Pennsylvania Game Commission in 1896 did things begin to change in favor of the deer.

Acorns are said to be a favorite food of whitetails, but upon examination of stomachs, they were found to eat 98 different plants. I admit that they have caused little damage in our yard. One severe winter, they ate three feet of ivy growing up the trunk of a maple tree at the corner of our house, but mostly they take a nip here, a bite there, and move on. Once, they did get their share of sweet corn, which prompted us to use vinyl deer fencing. Our daughter reminded us that one also ate all the yellow petunias around the mailbox but left the purple ones.

Male deer usually mate when two and a half years old, while females mate at one and a half years. After a gestation period of about six months, a single fawn is born to the first time mother. Afterwards, twins are usual, though sometimes the doe has triplets. The four to five pound babies learn early to obey their mother. She pushes them down with her muzzle into tall grass or brush where they should remain quiet until she returns from foraging. So well do their spotted coats blend with their surroundings, it takes a sharp eye to detect a hidden fawn. When our granddaughter's two little girls and their dad were picking raspberries in our berry patch, they didn't see a hidden fawn until it dashed away.

By late August, bucks have grown new antlers. Food and health, rather than age, determine the size of racks, especially of older bucks, biologists tell us. Through the rutting season, the bucks fight, and two are sometimes found with their antlers locked together, dead of starvation.

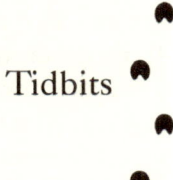

Tidbits

It isn't unusual to be surprised at Ivy Lane, and the surprise often leads us to go in search of information. Such was the case when I looked out the kitchen window and saw a rabbit gathering gobs of dried grass and leaves in her mouth. I use the female pronoun because it is known that the doe, the female rabbit, builds the nest, or bed, in which she gives birth to five or so babies. The rabbit I watched disappeared into the hedges but soon returned for more bedding. Several weeks later, I searched for, and found, the cozy bed she had made, but it had not been used. Cahalane states that it will not be used if disturbed even by mice, in fear that the disturber might be a predator and return. Nor is it used if made too early before the birth of the babies. The mother will make another one when the birth time draws nearer.

Seconds watching through the kitchen window sometimes present a sight never seen before. Recently, a young rabbit was eating grass and cracked corn near the ash tree feeder while a squirrel busily snatched sunflower seeds and ran off to bury them. Returning once from one of his forays, something triggered the squirrel to run directly toward the rabbit. The bunny must have been totally surprised, but at the last moment, he ran. Through the shrubbery, across the lawn, around the ash tree, he ran with the squirrel right behind him. Then, just as quickly as the chase started, it stopped. The squirrel returned to his business of burying seeds, but the rabbit scurried into the shrubbery. A bit later, a much larger rabbit appeared, and immediately Bunny popped out from hiding, and both rabbits began eating. Maybe the "buddy system" works for the rabbits, as the bushytail didn't interfere again.

—

Imagine, if you can, looking up into a tree in your home yard in the United States and seeing what looks like an iguana. That can't be, we told ourselves when it happened to us. That reptile is found "south of the border". After the stares, the denials, the can't be anything else, finally Van thought it might be, and the, "It is an iguana. An *iguana*," he emphasized.

Someone tired of such a pet, I assume, dropped the reptile off to fend for himself. He never came down where we could catch him, and when a cool fall spell arrived three or four days later, he disappeared.

AND OTHER CREATURES

Bufo the Toad

We have never known where the toads come from that appear in our garden. One was so small, maybe an inch long, that, according to what I've read, he was only six to eight weeks old. In *New Nature Library*, published in 1914, Mary C. Dickerson states that toadlets leave the water where they are hatched when about one half inch long. Therein lies my question. The nearest pond to our yard is about one quarter mile away. Did that tiny toad hop that distance in two months? How far from its birthplace will a toad travel?

Large toads like our garden, also. Late one afternoon, as I pulled weeds from around the carrots, a big toad hopped away. I was delighted to have him in the garden, for toads devour a great number of cutworms, caterpillars, slugs, and beetles—all injurious to gardeners' vegetables. Toads eat living, moving food, and woe to the bug that flies or crawls near. It has little chance of escaping the long, sticky tongue of *Bufo americanus*.

The morning after I found the toad, I looked for him near the carrots, but he was not there. "Look under that propped up board," my husband said, and there sat Bufo, his golden eyes wide open. Only once or twice all summer did he fail to return for the day to his sleeping quarters under the board.

A young growing toad sheds its skin often, but old toads shed their skins only four times a year. The skin is shed in one piece and swallowed by its owner, the entire process taking only about five minutes. I visited Bufo often hoping to see him shed his skin, but that must be a private matter for I never saw the act.

Summer passed. Nights chilled in autumn, and one morning the toad wasn't home. Nor the next. Nor was he under the board the third morning. "He's snuggled down deep in the ground for winter," my husband said.

—

Months later, spring arrived with clear, sunny days and warming temperatures. The beets and carrots kept growing, and I watched for the toad. Had he survived the ice storms and frozen landscape of our garden? I wondered for the days were getting longer, but then one morning, there he sat under the board. I told him I was glad to see him, that I hoped he would enjoy the insects hiding in our garden, and that I would see him almost every day. I did, until one morning I lifted the board to find a garter snake in Bufo's bed. A fat spot in the snake told the story. He had eaten Bufo.

"Get him out of the garden," I yelled at my husband. "Take him away." I was angry. I was hurt. That viper had eaten "my" toad, and I never wanted to see him again.

"No," my husband said. "He has just eaten, and he needs to stay quiet until he has digested his food. If he doesn't, he'll expel what he has eaten."

"Well, get him out of here soon," I said, emphasizing every word.

According to Charles Fergus in *Wildlife of Pennsylvania*, toads do have some protection from their predators. They can puff up to appear larger, which makes it difficult for some of their enemies to swallow them. They also have a kidney-shaped bump, a parotid gland, located behind each eye, which contains a strong steroid, strong enough to affect a predator's heart and blood pressure.

When we moved to Ivy Lane, I suspected that we would see snakes. The nearby field of blackberries, brown-eyed Susans, goldenrod, and other wild growing things was the perfect habitat for a black racer, I thought. All we ever saw was a small garter snake that sunned at the walkway step and now, maybe the same one had eaten my toad, and my husband was asking me to accept him as the predator he was.

I grew up where snakes, any kind, were detested and their heads chopped off with a hoe. My husband has tried to educate me along that line, and I can, at least, look at them as long as there is distance between us, but don't ask me to act normal when one slithers across the path at my feet.

When I expressed my concern about snakes, my husband said, "They'll get out of your way. I doubt you'll ever step on one," which is exactly what I had done as a child running barefoot through a field. I have never forgotten that awful squishy feeling.

Next morning, I hurried my husband to the garden to carry out my wishes, but the snake remained under the board. Two days later, I found him in the squash bed.

"Go away," I said. "Go look for mice or voles. I don't want to see you, EVER."

Accept predation? It's hard to do, sometimes.

—

WOOD FROG

On a late summer day as my husband and I stepped from the garden, a frog leaped toward the iris bed. He barely hesitated before leaping again, but the pause was long enough for us to identify him as a wood frog. We were quite surprised as wood frogs are considered inhabitants of moist woodlands. Our yard cannot be considered woods, though a "finger" of tangled vines and scrubby trees adjoin our acre. Shaded? Yes. Moist? Sometimes. Yet, there was a wood frog, not the first, but the second we had found in our yard.

My husband picked up our welcome visitor and put him in the garden. Perhaps he would eat a few slugs before succumbing to a long winter sleep.

As summer wanes and nights lengthen, breezes cool and insects disappear, *Rana sylvatica* searches for the right place in which to endure winter storms. Soon after the arrival of autumn, he crawls under an old log or merely snuggles under a few dead leaves. Either is scant cover for the frigid weather of the far north, but fear not for his safety.

"To survive freezing," says Charles Fergus, author of *Wildlife in Pennsylvania and the Northeast,* "they (wood frogs) produce large amounts of glucose, which acts as a natural antifreeze to keep ice from rupturing body cells."

In March, or sometimes February, the frogs emerge from their winter beds and go in search of water. Even though ponds may remain icy, males and females congregate. About two inches long, head and body, the males are one of the first frogs to voice their awakening. Their hoarse calls have been likened to the quacking of ducks, but never mind how it sounds to the human ear. To the silent female frog, it's an invitation to mate, and the icy water is of no consequence.

Females, larger than males by an inch, lay masses of eggs which resemble "clear tapioca pudding", says Scott Shalaway, nature writer. Eggs may hatch in two weeks, but if temperatures drop, hatching may be delayed for as long as a month. The embryos simply quit growing until the weather warms.

The first eggs laid have a distinct advantage over later ones laid because those in the center of the egg mass remain warmer than the outer ones. The earlier hatching of the center eggs gives those tadpoles an advantage also, as they eat the newly hatched ¼ inch long tadpoles of the outer, cooler edge of the mass.

Wood frogs don't hang around to see their offspring grow up. According to Mary C. Dickerson, a biologist of the early 20th century, the species "is more of a land creature than one of water". She added, "It is to the ground what the chickadee is to the trees—a gentle spirit of the woods," so as soon as mating is over and eggs are laid, adults leave the pools. Their wanderings may take them far from water, which can account for the one in our yard that September day.

BUTTERFLIES

"Van, did you put a butterfly on the window?" I called to my husband one February morning as I walked into the living room. My immediate thought was that he had placed one of his pinned specimens there to tease me, but as he bounded into the living room, I knew he had not.

At that moment, the butterfly lifted its wings as if about to take off. It was alive!

"I must have brought a chrysalis in on that last fireplace wood," my astounded husband said as he admired the beautiful yellow and black swallowtail.

What a surprise on a winter day! Though we tried to lure the butterfly to our poorly constructed artificial flower and sugar water, our attempt was futile.

Butterflies are some of America's most beautiful insects, and the tiger swallowtail, with yellow wings edged in black, is a favorite. Sipping nectar from a specially planted butterfly bush, or even the common garden phlox, the lovely creatures are almost sure to attract attention. They gather at mud puddles or rotting fruit, and serious butterfly watchers have found that a paper butterfly will serve as a lure, also.

Butterflies lay eggs, which hatch into larvae called caterpillars. Each larval species has preferred plants on which they like to feed just as you and I have favorite foods. It is on these special plants that the female butterfly lays her eggs. While carrot and parsley leaves are favorites of the black-tailed swallowtail larvae, the tiger swallowtail likes the leaves of the ash and birch trees in our yard.

Butterflies have many enemies during all of their life stages. Birds eat both larvae and adults, and insects destroy many larvae, also. Caterpillars on our tomato leaves often have tiny white cocoons sticking to their backs.

Those are the eggs or egg skins of parasites. When the eggs hatch, the tiny flies or wasps bore into the caterpillar to feed on its juices. Soon it dies.

However, according to a biologist in Louisiana who studied Mexico's Ross's metalmark butterfly for 25 years or longer, a strange relationship exists between that species and another insect, the carpenter ant.

Soon after a metalmark egg hatches, the larva begins to produce a sweet fluid called honeydew. Carpenter ants feed on the fluid without harming the larva and in exchange protect the larva from its enemies. The ants dig a small hole at the base of the food plant and coax the caterpillar down into it each morning. They cover it with tiny dirt pellets, but at dusk, they reopen the hole. Before permitting their captive to climb the plant to feed, the ants scout out the plant and squirt formic acid to drive away or kil, any enemies. Only then do they "herd" the larva back to its feeding station for the night. When morning comes, it is tucked away again in its earthen bed by the ants. (National Wildlife Magazine August-September 1988)

Mimicry is a way some butterflies have of protecting themselves. Through the millions of years that the insects have been around, some have evolved to look like what they aren't. Angle wings are primarily forest dwellers. When resting on a twig with wings folded above the body, the butterfly is so much like a dead leaf that its enemies never notice it.

The red-spotted purple mimics the pipevine swallowtail whose larvae feed on plants distasteful to birds, so both species are left alone. The viceroy is a look-alike of the bad tasting monarch, so it escapes birds, too, but the tradeoff of looks for safety is carried even further with this species. Its chrysalis, the stage between the larva and the adult, resembles a bird dropping and is passed over by its enemies.

Don't be surprised if you see a butterfly, such as the mourning cloak my husband and I saw one January day, flitting over the snow. While most winter over as chrysalides, some adults pass the cold months hibernating in rotten logs, beneath tree bark or even the shingles on a house. The mourning cloak may take a short flight on a sunny winter day but returns to its hiding place as the day grows chilly.

Some species choose yet another way to cope with winter. Migration has been defined as a seasonal movement, usually on an annual cycle, of animals which leave, and return to, their breeding areas. Birds are the best-known migrants, but some insects are migratory also.

The reddish-orange monarch butterfly is the long-distance traveler of the butterfly world. Eastern broods, drifting south through autumn skies, are headed for their wintering grounds in central Mexico, where local residents of one area say they are the souls of dead children going to heaven.

—

Though some never reach the high mountain area, hordes arrive to cluster on fir trees.

On their way to Mexico, the monarchs stop to rest and sip nectar from autumn flowers. A single head of goldenrod or fall aster may hold half a dozen, but they are in little danger of being eaten. Birds learned long ago to leave the monarch alone because its larvae feed on poisonous plants, which give the butterfly a foul taste.

It had been known for years that west coast butterflies wintered in California, but not until 1976 did scientists determine where the eastern and central North American migrants ended their journey. Even there, in the Mexican mountains, life is not assured. Many die in the winter cold, and there are some scientists who believe that thousands may perish with every drop of one degree of temperature. Yet, every spring, those that do survive begin their trek northward.

Early in the journey, the reproduction process begins, and it is the progeny of the winter survivors that eventually end up as far north as Canada. By September, adults of eggs laid in July and August are heading south again, and it is then that our daughter in Minnesota calls.

"Mom, our yard is full of monarchs," she says. "They are all over the trees and shrubs."

Next day she calls again. "They're gone," she says. "This morning as the air warmed they left, all of them, going south."

Butterflies captured the interest of the early Europeans who arrived in America, also. In *The Butterfly Book*, by W. J. Holland, the author relates an interesting historical story of the tiger swallowtail.

In 1587, Sir Walter Raleigh sent a third group of English colonists to America with John White, an artist, as their leader. On that trip, or a previous one, for White had sailed to the "New World" before, someone gave to him, or showed him, a tiger swallowtail butterfly, which he sketched. Leaving the colonists at Roanoke, then considered to be in Virginia but now in North Carolina, White returned to England for supplies and gave the sketch to someone there.

Upon his return to America in 1590, White found only a single trace of the Roanoke colonists, the word "Croatoun" (as spelled by Holland) carved on a tree. The entire group, including White's daughter, her husband, Ananias Dare, and their baby daughter, Virginia Dare, the first child born of English parents in America, had disappeared.

Meanwhile in England, White's butterfly sketch was in good hands, and at his writing, according to Holland, it remained safe in the English Museum, a reminder of John White, the artist, his beloved family, and America's "Lost Colony".

FIREFLIES

Van and I sit outside near the garden, watching fireflies and a single bat, a little brown bat, we guess. The first firefly flash is at the phlox, and I can see the insect as it flies away. Then flashes appear at the corner of the garden and all around us. There are bigger flashes, I tell Van, under the maple tree in our neighbor's yard. He is quiet.

Some flashes are higher now, as high as the corn, even the pole bean stakes, but they fade out as they ascend toward the light sky right above us. Will the bat eat the beetles, the maker of those flashes, I wonder.

These light-making flyers are in the final stage of a complete metamorphosis. From eggs larvae emerge, which also produce light and are known as glow worms. Larvae become pupae, and pupae transform into adults. During their one week of adulthood as flashers, they eat nothing. They are too busy flashing their lights to induce females to respond. The right kind of female, that is, one of their own species. There are more than 30 species in our northeastern states, and the females of some species are well, shall we say, assassins. They can mimic the flash pattern of rival female species, thus attracting the males of that species. Not knowing he is doomed, the male pays her a visit only to be eaten.

We move from our garden spot to the back porch to see what is going on in another area of our yard. Fireflies are there, also. Unlike our man-made lights, which consist of much heat, beetle lights are almost all light and no heat, and some of these flashes appear much brighter and larger.

"Are they the flashes of the beetle species which have two abdominal segments of luminescence instead of one?" I wonder aloud.

Van is non-committal. He is a scientist and requires "proof-positive" for identification, which led us to the Smithsonian insect collection during

—

our honeymoon. There Dr. Chapin (I'm sorry I don't know his first name) took me aside to show me the most beautiful insects I have ever seen while my new husband studied fungus beetles in order to identify one he had found recently.

The second night of porch watching, the phone rang as we were about to step out into the darkness. I answered the phone and, regretfully, missed the following:

From Van's journal: July 17th

> "About 8:15 I took my tea out on the back porch to enjoy the great weather we've been having. Just before deep dusk I saw a large striped skunk trot into the yard from somewhere near the garage and head for the 'critter food', tail held high. I didn't have a flashlight, but I could follow the skunk because of his white stripes and the light underside of his tail. I became aware of the strange actions of the skunk for his tail was still up—a sure sign of warning, and his odor was becoming more noticeable. Then I caught a flash of movement, and something moved between the skunk and me. It went to the hosta pool (wildlife water), and I got enough of a silhouette to recognize a raccoon. Fair size. I'm not sure if he took a drink, but he came back passing the skunk by 3 ft. or so. At that moment, the skunk lunged at the raccoon and he left the yard in a hurry."

July 31st,

> "We have not seen the raccoon again, but we continue to watch fireflies."

The season will progress, and the nocturnal chorus of katydids and crickets will assure us that all is well in their world, and life goes on. Avian migrants will be going south soon, some of them for the first time, including the young catbirds that fledged from a nest in the forsythia. Life goes on for them also. For Van and me it is the same.

Thirty-five years ago, we realized that the diverse habitat of this one acre on Ivy Lane would provide us the opportunity to explore the many small worlds that surround us. We need not now travel afar, but are content to stay at home and enjoy the natural world that is a part of our everyday life. We are still exploring.

Resources:

Books I have enjoyed and from which I have learned.

Field Guide to the Birds of North America, National Geographic Society.

The Peterson Fieldguides.

Birds of America, Editor-in-Chief T. Gilbert Pearson, Garden City Books, Garden City, NY.

The Warblers of America, Edited by Ludlow Griscom, Doubleday Company, Inc., Garden City, NY.

The Book of Owls, Lewis Wayne Walker, Alfred A. Knopf, NY.

Wildlife of Pennsylvania and the Northeast, Charles Fergus, Stackpole Books, Mechanicsburg, PA.

Mammals of North America, Victor H. Cahalane, Macmillan Company, NY.

Mammals of North America, Roland W. Kays and Don E. Wilson, Princeton University Press, Princeton, NJ.

Mammals of the Eastern United States, William J. Hamilton, Jr. and John O. Whitaker, Jr., Comstock Publishing Associates, a division of Cornell University Press, Ithaca, NY. and London, England.

Insects, Borror, Triplehorn and Johnson, Saunders College Publishing.

—

The Butterfly Book, W.J. Holland, Doubleday and Company, Inc., NY.

Nature's Events, John Serrao, Stackpole Books, Mechanicsburg, PA.

Winter World, Bernd Heinrich, HarperCollins Publishers, New York, NY.

From Laurel Hill to Siler's Bog: the Walking Adventures of a Naturalist, John K. Terres, Alfred A. Kopf, NY.

Those of the Forest, Wallace Byron Grange, Willow Creek Press, Minocqua, Wisconsin.

A Valley Called Canaan: 1885-2002, Edwin Daryl Michael, McClain Printing Company, Parsons, WV.

Living on the Wind, Scott Weidensaul, North Point Press, San Francisco, CA.

Thank you, Authors, and many others too numerous to name,
for enriching my life.

www.ingramcontent.com/pod-product-compliance
Lightning Source LLC
Chambersburg PA
CBHW030403290526
45785CB00004B/1891